FIRST
MEALS

FIRST MEALS

Fast, Healthy, and Fun Foods to Tempt Infants and Toddlers
from Baby's First Foods to Favorite Family Feasts

ANNABEL KARMEL

A DK PUBLISHING BOOK

A DK PUBLISHING BOOK

www.dk.com

Project Editor
Lorna Damms

Deputy Art Director
Carole Ash

US Editors
Iris Rosoff &
Joan Whitman

Managing Editors
Corinne Roberts &
Mary Ling

Art Editors
Carmel O'Neill & Emy Manby

Consultant Editor
(on child development)
Caroline Greene

Senior Art Editor
Carole Oliver

DTP Designer
Bridget Roseberry

Food Photography
Ian O'Leary

Production Manager
Maryann Rogers

Model Photography
Andy Crawford

Production Controller
Martin Croshaw

Home Economist
Janice Murfitt

Note on the nutritional breakdowns of recipes:
all information is approximate and based on figures from food composition tables, not on direct analysis of made up dishes. Thus analyses should be used as a guide, not as guaranteed figures. Some ingredients are not specified by weight, so an estimated weight has been used. No analyses have been provided for recipe variations. Analyses are per portion.

As many vitamins are destroyed when exposed to air or light, the guidelines on rich sources apply to dishes served immediately after preparation. Where recipes are frozen immediately, they will, in general, still provide a useful amount of the nutrients indicated. The wording "Rich source" has been based on both absolute values and values when compared to the energy (Cal) content of the recipe.

First American Edition 1999
4 6 8 10 9 7 5 3

Published in the United States by DK Publishing, Inc.,
95 Madison Avenue, New York, New York 10016

Library of Congress Cataloging-in-Publication Data

Karmel, Annabel
First Meals / Annabel Karmel. -- 1st American ed.
         p.   cm.
Includes index.
ISBN 0-7894-4177-2
1. Infants -- Nutrition -- Popular works. 2. Toddlers -- Nutrition -- Popular works. I. Title.
RJ206.K246   1999   98-39276
641.5'622--dc21   CIP

Reproduced in Italy by GRB
Printed and bound in China by L.Rex Printing Co., Ltd.

CONTENTS

4–6 MONTHS

A guide to successful weaning, with advice on introducing solids, and featuring a photographic gallery of first purees and 14 simple recipes.

6–9 MONTHS

Expert information on introducing new tastes and textures, followed by a gallery of more advanced purees and 27 recipes.

Introduction

When it comes to the health and happiness of their child, I think that all parents will agree that only the very best will do. I lost my first child, Natasha, at the heartbreakingly early age of 13 weeks after she contracted a viral infection. Though this illness was not diet-related, Natasha's loss made me even more determined to give my second child, Nicholas, the best possible start in life. It was Nicholas who gave me my first experience of coping with a fussy eater. Indeed, my interest in the whole subject of child nutrition was born out of my own frustrations with feeding a child who, for a time, would eat only a limited range of foods. Thus the strategies and solutions for common eating problems that are presented in this book are based not only on current nutritional guidelines but on experience and a deep conviction that food is one of the best forms of preventive medicine.

❖

At a time when diet is most crucial to health, we should not be reliant upon processed foods from jars and packages. After all, there is no great mystique to making baby food and there is nothing better for your child than home-cooked food made from fresh ingredients. Home cooking is an economical option and, as the recipes in this book show, it need not be time-consuming. There are many excellent purees that do not involve cooking and other recipes suitable for batch-cooking and freezing that enable a whole month's food supply to be prepared in just a couple of hours. These homemade meals accustom babies to the natural variations in taste of freshly cooked food, and this helps them adapt to family meals and grow up to be less fussy eaters. So while parents are giving their baby the best nutritional start in life, they are also helping guard against future eating difficulties.

Unfortunately, for many children convenience and junk foods are a
regular part of their diet: fewer and fewer families are sitting down to
meals together. Instead, children are often raised on a depressingly familiar
repertoire of processed, packaged foods and "TV dinners" – pizzas, chicken
nuggets, fries, and spaghetti hoops. It can seem that "real" food is only for
adults, and that children have a special diet consisting of some of the
poorest quality, most unhealthy food around. Yet parents are the ones in
charge of what their children eat, and it is up to parents to give their
children the opportunity to follow a varied, healthy diet.

❖

My three children, Nicholas, Lara, and Scarlett, have been my constant
inspiration over the years, but I am also grateful to all the babies and young
children who have contributed to my research into nutrition and development,
albeit unknowingly, and tested my new recipes. Children are exacting critics
and while they are rarely interested in whether their food is healthy, they
do care if it tastes good. Accordingly, the recipes in this book are designed
to combine "child appeal" with sound nutritional principles.
I hope that many of them will be firm family favorites for years to come.

Annabel Karmel.

Early Nutrition

A BALANCED DIET is one that perfectly suits your growing child's needs. Breast milk or formula is an essential source of nourishment throughout the first year of your baby's life, but from the time you begin weaning him, you should work toward establishing a diet that provides the five essential nutrients: carbohydrates, vitamins, fat, minerals, and protein. Remember that your child's needs are different than your own. The average adult is advised to follow a high-fiber, low-fat diet, but the under 5s need significantly more fat and concentrated sources of calories and nutrients to fuel their rapid growth during the early years.

Your baby's milk

Throughout his first 6 months, your baby is totally dependent on breast milk or formula for all his nutritional needs. Although you may have begun weaning your baby at 4 or 5 months, his initial solid intake is so small that these "real" foods are little more than a taste experience, and it is vital not to reduce his milk. Once your baby is 6 months old, you can introduce small quantities of whole milk in cooking and with breakfast cereals. Once he reaches his first birthday, whole milk can become his usual drink, but until then he needs the vitamins and iron found in breast milk or formula.

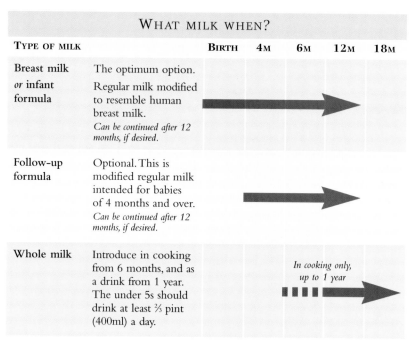

WHAT MILK WHEN?

TYPE OF MILK		BIRTH	4M	6M	12M	18M
Breast milk or infant formula	The optimum option. Regular milk modified to resemble human breast milk. *Can be continued after 12 months, if desired.*					
Follow-up formula	Optional. This is modified regular milk intended for babies of 4 months and over. *Can be continued after 12 months, if desired.*					
Whole milk	Introduce in cooking from 6 months, and as a drink from 1 year. The under 5s should drink at least ⅔ pint (400ml) a day.				*In cooking only, up to 1 year*	

Water

Babies are vulnerable to dehydration, so it is essential to maintain their fluid intake. If your baby is breast-fed, milk will supply the necessary fluids, but bottle-fed babies may need sips of water since formula is not so thirst-quenching. Once your baby is on a mainly solid diet, you will need to increase his fluid intake. Cooled boiled tap water is inexpensive, accessible, and the best thirst-quencher. Young babies will need only a few sips of water, but it is wise to encourage your child to drink water from an early age: although there are many herbal and fruit drinks marketed for babies, most contain sugar, which can harm developing teeth and give your baby a taste for sweet drinks. Do not give mineral water or use it in feedings: it is not bacteriologically safe unless boiled and may contain a higher level of sodium than is recommended for babies.

FAT

THE SOURCES OF SATURATED FAT: meat ◆ butter and margarine ◆ lard ◆ eggs ◆ cheese ◆ hydrogenated vegetable fat or oil, found in processed foods such as cookies.

THE SOURCES OF UNSATURATED FAT: olive oil ◆ sunflower oil ◆ corn oil ◆ sesame oil ◆ safflower oil ◆ oily fish.

FAT is vital to growth. Saturated fat is derived mainly from animal sources and processed foods containing vegetable fat; unsaturated fat is derived from vegetable and fish sources. Saturated fats can increase blood cholesterol levels, and high intakes are linked to heart disease in adults. While you should make sure that there is enough fat in your child's diet, it is a good idea to encourage healthy eating by choosing lean meat and using vegetable oils rather than butter for frying. Milk and cheese contain saturated fats, but are also a good source of calcium, protein, and vitamins. Children between the ages of 2 and 5 should get up to 35 percent of their total energy intake from fat. Up to the age of 1, children should derive 50 percent of their energy from fat.

PROTEIN

THE SOURCES OF PROTEIN: red meat ◆ poultry ◆ liver ◆ fish ◆ eggs ◆ milk ◆ cheese (but not cream cheese) ◆ grains ◆ legumes ◆ seeds.

PROTEIN is essential for growth and repair of body tissues; if we have an inadequate level of protein, our resistance to disease and infection is lowered. Protein is made up of amino acids, some of which the body can manufacture, and some of which must be obtained from food. Animal proteins, including milk, contain all the amino acids the body needs, but soy is the only plant-based food that contains all these essential amino acids. Other foods must be combined in order to provide complete proteins. For example, grains can be combined with legumes or with a very small quantity of animal protein to provide a complete protein. Because protein is not stored by the body, foods containing protein should be eaten on most days. However, protein-rich foods should not be the major part of a baby's meal since a high-protein diet can put a strain on immature kidneys. Protein deficiency is almost unheard of in the West.

CARBOHYDRATE

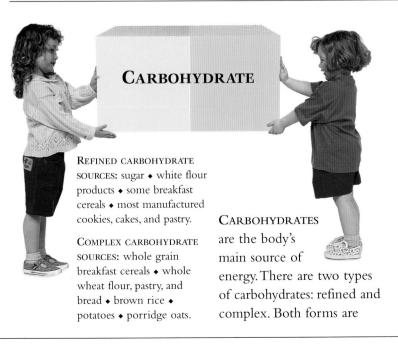

REFINED CARBOHYDRATE SOURCES: sugar ◆ white flour products ◆ some breakfast cereals ◆ most manufactured cookies, cakes, and pastry.

COMPLEX CARBOHYDRATE SOURCES: whole grain breakfast cereals ◆ whole wheat flour, pastry, and bread ◆ brown rice ◆ potatoes ◆ porridge oats.

CARBOHYDRATES are the body's main source of energy. There are two types of carbohydrates: refined and complex. Both forms are converted into blood sugar, thereby providing energy (calories). Refined carbohydrates, such as white bread and most store cookies, are made up of ingredients that are stripped of their natural fiber during processing and have lost most of their valuable nutrients. Complex carbohydrates are energy-rich foods that retain their vitamins, minerals, and fiber and are therefore more useful to the body. This form of carbohydrates should make up about 60 percent of your child's diet.

CALCIUM

CALCIUM is important for the health and formation of bones and teeth. Two thirds of a pint (400ml) of milk a day provides enough calcium for children between the ages of 1 and 5.

THE SOURCES OF CALCIUM: milk ◆ cheese ◆ yogurt ◆ leafy vegetables ◆ tofu ◆ nuts ◆ sardines ◆ sesame seeds.

ZINC

ZINC is essential for normal growth and for the efficient function of the immune system. A varied diet should provide all the body's daily needs.

THE SOURCES OF ZINC: shellfish ◆ red meat ◆ peanuts ◆ sunflower seeds ◆ fortified breakfast cereals.

VITAMINS

VITAMINS are essential for the maintenance of a healthy body. Vitamins are either water-soluble (B complex and C) or fat-soluble (A, D, E, and K). Water-soluble vitamins are destroyed by heat and, as their name indicates, dissolve in water, so foods rich in these vitamins should not be overcooked. Fat-soluble vitamins are stored in the body and may be harmful in large doses. Current guidelines recommend that all children under 5 take a supplement of vitamins A, C, and D.

VITAMIN A (including beta-carotene and retinol) is essential for growth, fighting infection, healthy skin, good vision, and strong bones. Good sources of retinol are: liver, eggs. Beta-carotene is an antioxidant that helps to protect against disease. Good sources are: carrots, red peppers, corn, tomatoes, sweet potatoes, melons, apricots, mangoes.

B COMPLEX VITAMINS, including folic acid, are needed for growth, a healthy nervous system, and to aid digestion. Good sources are: meat, especially liver, tofu, sardines, eggs, nuts, dark green vegetables, dairy produce, whole grain cereals, avocados, bananas.

VITAMIN C is required for growth, tissue repair, healthy skin, and to aid iron absorption. Good sources are: citrus fruits, strawberries, kiwis, dark green leafy vegetables, potatoes, peppers.

VITAMIN D is manufactured by skin exposed to sunlight, and is needed to absorb calcium and phosphorous for healthy bones and teeth. Good sources are: salmon, tuna, sardines, milk, cheese, eggs.

VITAMIN E is needed for the maintenance of the body's cell structure and it helps the body create and maintain red blood cells. Good sources are: vegetable oils, wheat germ, avocados, nuts.

IRON

THE SOURCES OF IRON: red meat, particularly liver ◆ oily fish ◆ legumes ◆ fortified infant rice ◆ fortified breakfast cereals ◆ bread ◆ green leafy vegetables ◆ dried fruit, especially dried apricots.

IRON is needed for both physical and mental development. Babies are born with a supply of iron that lasts for about 6 months. After this time it is important to make sure they get the iron they need from their solids because iron deficiency, which can lead to anemia if unchecked, leaves children feeling run-down and tired. A baby's iron requirements are particularly high between the ages of 6 and 12 months. Premature babies are especially vulnerable to iron depletion since their supply of iron may last for only 6 weeks. If your baby was born prematurely, you may be advised by your doctor to give him an iron supplement until he is 1 year old. (See page 53 for further information.)

FOOD ALLERGIES & INTOLERANCE

WHAT IS A FOOD ALLERGY?

An allergic reaction occurs when the immune system perceives a harmless substance as a threat and overreacts, triggering unpleasant, occasionally dangerous, side effects. Because young babies' immune systems are not fully developed, they are more likely to become sensitized to common allergens, such as eggs and gluten. This is why the introduction of these foods should be delayed. Children who do experience a food allergy may outgrow it by the age of 3, but occasionally an allergy will persist and the only option is avoidance. If you suspect that your child is allergic to a common food such as milk or wheat (see below), seek expert advice on planning your child's diet.

A FAMILY HISTORY OF ALLERGIES

If your family has a history of food allergy or atopic disease (e.g., hay fever, asthma, urticaria, or eczema) it is recommended that your baby be exclusively breast-fed for the first 4–6 months, and that foods likely to cause an allergy are not introduced before 6 months at the earliest. Begin weaning with low-allergen foods, such as rice, potato, pear, and apple, and introduce foods one at a time so that any adverse reactions can be traced to the "trigger" food. It can be difficult to pinpoint which, if any, foods provoke an allergic response and it should be remembered that other factors besides food (such as house dust, pets, detergents, or bath products) can trigger these reactions. If there is a history of allergy to

a particular food, avoid that food until your child is at least 1 year old, but never remove key foods from your child's diet without first consulting a doctor.

COW'S MILK (PROTEIN) ALLERGY

An allergic reaction to one of the proteins found in cow's milk, cow's milk-based infant formulas, and dairy products can give rise to diverse symptoms, namely diarrhea, vomiting, abdominal pains, eczema, and lactose intolerance (see below). Babies who experience this allergic reaction can be given a soy-based or hypoallergenic formula, on the advice of a doctor, if breast milk is not an option. Older children need a dairy-free diet (consult a doctor or dietitian).

NUT ALLERGY

Although allergy to tree nuts is relatively rare, the peanut is the trigger for one of the most severe allergic reactions, anaphylactic shock (in which the throat swells and breathing becomes difficult). In families with a history of any kind of food allergy, it is advisable to avoid all products containing peanuts or unrefined peanut oil until the child is 3 years old. If there is no history of allergy, peanuts of a suitable consistency (e.g., smooth peanut butter) can be introduced from 6 months.

LACTOSE INTOLERANCE

Lactose is the sugar in milk and lactose intolerance is the inability to digest this sugar because of a lack of a digestive enzyme, called lactase, in the gut. The condition, whose main

symptom is diarrhea, is usually caused by gastroenteritis bacteria or viruses damaging the gut where lactase is produced. Once the gut has recovered and repaired the damage (which may take anywhere from a few days to a few weeks), the enzyme will be produced once more and the intolerance will then disappear. While the condition lasts, it can be managed by using either a soy-based formula (which can be bought from most stores) or a low-lactose infant formula.

GLUTEN INTOLERANCE

Wheat, barley, oats, and their products contain gluten, and this substance can provoke similar symptoms to lactose intolerance. Gluten intolerance may coexist with lactose intolerance and result from gut damage after an attack of gastroenteritis. Foods containing gluten should not be introduced into any baby's diet before 6 months. Gluten-free cereals, such as rice, millet, and corn, can be introduced from 4 months. If there is a family history of gluten intolerance, your baby should follow a gluten-free diet for at least the first year. In most cases, the condition disappears once the gut has had time to recover from the gastroenteritic illness. Chronic gluten intolerance is celiac disease. This condition requires proper dietary management, if diagnosed. It is thought that the availability of the more highly modified whey-based infant formulas and the later introduction of solid foods has led to a dramatic drop in the incidence of celiac disease.

Pantry

A WELL-STOCKED PANTRY is an invaluable asset to any kitchen. If you haven't had time to go shopping, you can use ingredients that are already on hand in the pantry to make a quick and nutritious meal for your children, or indeed for the whole family. While the lists of foods on these pages are by no means exhaustive, they represent a useful and versatile selection of staples that can be used as the basis for a wide range of dishes.

Dried staple foods

Bread and other grain products, such as pasta and rice, are invaluable carbohydrate sources that can be used as the basis for many quick, healthy meals. Although dried beans and legumes generally require some advance preparation, they are both nutritious and economical. In addition to the items listed right, stock: All-purpose flour • self-rising flour • whole wheat flour • cornstarch • taco shells • Chinese noodles.

BREAD PRODUCTS such as whole wheat and white bread, bread sticks, muffins.

BEANS AND LEGUMES, for example, red kidney beans, red and green lentils, haricot beans.

RICE, particularly infant rice for purees, white and brown long-grain rice, Arborio rice.

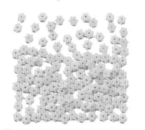

PASTA, including soup pasta, farfalle and fusilli, spaghetti, lasagna sheets, cannelloni tubes.

COUSCOUS and other wheat products, such as semolina and bulgur wheat.

DRIED FRUIT, including apricots, mangoes, peaches, prunes, apple rings, raisins.

Breakfast cereals

Choose low-sugar cereals made with rice, oats, or wheat. A whole grain variety is preferable, but avoid bran-based products with added fiber. Alternatively, make a mixed-grain muesli. Use fresh or dried fruits, rather than refined sugar, to sweeten cereals.

COMMERCIAL CEREALS, with a low sugar content, for instance, cornflakes, puffed rice, and wheat flakes.

MUESLI, made with a mixture of rolled oats, mixed grains, toasted wheat germ, and chopped dried fruit.

HIDDEN SUGARS

◆ BREAKFAST CEREALS may contain more than 45 percent sugar in different forms, e.g., maltose, honey, glucose, and dextrose, and these may be listed separately, making it harder to judge the total content.

Dairy products

Choose pasteurized whole milk and dairy products for children under 5 years old.

CHEESES such as soft cream cheese for dips and spreads; mild or medium Cheddar, Edam, or Gruyère; cottage cheese; fresh Parmesan.

MILK should be whole and pasteurized. Keep a package of powdered whole milk in the kitchen cabinet as a staple ingredient.

YOGURT, particularly a creamy, mild-tasting, regular plain yogurt; low-sugar fruit or vanilla yogurt; fromage frais.

BUTTER (a sweet or lightly salted variety) or a good quality margarine for spreading on bread or for shallow frying and baking.

Sauces, oils & seasonings

A good supply of bottled sauces and oils, herbs, and spices will give plenty of culinary scope.

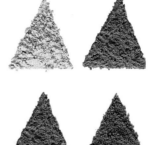

SAUCES & FLAVORINGS such as soy sauce, oyster sauce, tomato paste, Worcestershire sauce, pesto, vegetable and chicken bouillon.

OILS & VINEGARS for cooking and salad dressings, including olive oil, sunflower oil, vegetable oil, sesame oil, balsamic and wine vinegars.

HERBS, for example, mixed dried herbs, bay leaves, oregano, thyme, prepared bouquets garnis, fresh basil, fresh and dried parsley.

SPICES such as powdered cinnamon and ginger for baking; nutmeg (buy the whole spice); fresh ginger; mild paprika; chili powder.

Frozen foods

Many vegetables and fruits such as peas and berries are frozen within 2–3 hours of being picked, ensuring that they retain valuable nutrients. In fact, fresh vegetables that are stored for several days often contain fewer nutrients than frozen vegetables. Frozen chicken portions and fish fillets are good standbys. If buying breaded fish fillets, choose larger portions since there will be less coating in proportion to fish. Freeze bread and butter for emergencies and ice cream for quick desserts.

Canned foods

Some canned processed foods are high in sugar, salt, and saturated fat, so always read labels carefully. However, many canned products are valuable nutritionally. Stock: canned tuna • sardines • baked beans • kidney beans • plum tomatoes • corn.

Equipment

YOU WILL PROBABLY find that you already have most of the equipment needed to make home-cooked meals for your child, but certain items will facilitate food preparation and prove useful for general family cooking. Equipment does not need to be expensive or complicated, but you should look for items that will make preparing solids easy for you and that will later help your baby learn how to feed himself.

Processors & blenders

Electric food processors or hand blenders make it easy to puree large quantities of food quickly. Some foods, such as cooked apples, will puree to a smooth consistency in a blender or processor; other foods may need to be strained after pureeing.

MINI PROCESSORS are useful for making baby foods in small portions.

LARGE PROCESSORS facilitate cooking in batches, but a mini bowl attachment will work better for small quantities.

MOULIS puree foods while removing any indigestible husks or skins.

HAND-HELD BLENDERS are easy to clean and ideal for pureeing small quantities in the container provided with the blender.

MINI BOWL

A METAL-MESH strainer can be used to eliminate any fibrous material from purees for babies.

Freezer containers

Tiny portions of puree for babies can be frozen in ice cube trays (see page 18). You can also buy small containers that hold larger portions. These can go straight from the freezer to the microwave. Mini freezer and yogurt containers are also useful.

ICE CUBE TRAY made of flexible plastic allows you to freeze meal-size portions.

FREEZER CONTAINERS with snap-on lids are easily transported.

Steamers

A multilayered steamer allows you to cook several foods simultaneously. A collapsible steamer that fits different size pots is a versatile alternative.

STACKED STEAMER

COLLAPSIBLE STEAMER

Baby chairs

A bouncy chair that supports the back is ideal for the early stages of feeding. At around 6 months, your baby will probably then progress to a regular high chair with a safety strap. A clip-on chair with a safety strap is a lightweight, transportable, and space-saving option.

CLIP-ON CHAIRS may be clamped to a sturdy table that can take the extra weight. Do not clamp them over a cloth.

BOUNCY CHAIRS are lightweight seats that are ideal for babies who cannot yet sit unaided.

HIGH CHAIRS should be wide-based and sturdy, with a washable tray.

Feeding kit

There are many varieties of feeding bowls and spoons available. All that is needed to start with is a small bowl and a shallow weaning spoon, preferably one made of soft, flexible plastic that will not hurt tender gums. Later on, bowls with suction pads or with thermal linings, training cups, and cutlery designed especially for children become useful.

BOWLS should be made of heat-proof plastic. Choose one with a hand grip.

HEAT-SENSITIVE BOWLS and spoons change color to indicate if food is too hot.

SUCTION PADS on bowls allow them to be secured to high chair trays.

WEANING SPOON

WEANING SPOONS should have a small shallow bowl with no hard edges.

NIPPLE

Lid —

SOFT SPOUT

GRADUATED TRAINING CUP

TRAINING CUP

Rigid spout

TRAINING CUPS enable babies to take fluids independently. Most babies graduate from bottles to cups with a short spout and snap-tight lid and then to a regular cup.

Bibs

Feeding can be a messy business for young babies, their parents, and even the surrounding wallpaper. Protect your baby's clothes from the worst of the mess with bibs, and use a large, square, easy-to-wipe plastic mat, or just an old plastic tablecloth, under feeding chairs.

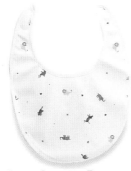

SOFT COTTON BIBS should have plastic backing and a velcro fastener.

PLASTIC BIBS with a molded trough are suitable for older babies.

BIBS WITH SLEEVES and ties at the back give the best protection.

Preparing Baby Food

YOU DON'T NEED any special expertise to prepare baby foods, but there are ways to streamline the process so that even busy parents can make foods that suit their baby's needs. Many first foods, such as mashed banana and avocado, make excellent baby purees and do not require any cooking. For other meals, you can either set aside unseasoned portions of food, such as vegetables, that are being cooked for the rest of the family, or cook batches of pureed foods specifically for your baby. The cooking methods shown on these two pages are useful for making the smooth purees suitable for the early stages of weaning (see pages 28–31 for recipes).

DIFFERENT COOKING TECHNIQUES

◆ STEAMING helps preserve the taste and nutrient content of fresh food. The water-soluble vitamins B and C can be destroyed by overcooking: broccoli loses 60 percent of its vitamin C boiled, 20 percent steamed.

◆ BOILING can destroy nutrients, so ingredients should be cooked until just tender in the minimum amount of water. Be careful not to overcook.

◆ MICROWAVING allows fast cooking of fruits and vegetables (and later fish) with minimal nutrient loss. When fresh ingredients are cooked rapidly at full power, most of the nutrients are retained.

◆ BAKING is a nutrient-retaining, labor-saving cooking method. Potatoes, sweet potatoes, and squash can be washed, pricked with a fork, and baked until tender. The flesh can then be scooped out and mashed.

Blending purees

2 Process the food until a smooth, even-textured puree is produced. If necessary, add a little of the cooking water to thin the mixture, then pulse briefly.

1 Cook small pieces of vegetable or fruit until tender. Drain, retaining a tablespoon or two of the cooking liquid, then pour into the food processor bowl.

3 The final texture of the puree should be completely smooth. It can be thinned with cooled boiled water for young babies.

Making purees with a mouli

1 To make a puree from fibrous ingredients, e.g., peas, fit the fine mouli blade, then place all the puree ingredients in the mouli and set it over a bowl.

Rotate the handle to push the pulp through the blades

Ingredients should be chopped into fairly uniform pieces

2 Turn the mouli handle to rotate the blade. Continue the grinding until most of the ingredients are pushed through the mouli, then discard the fibrous pulp left behind.

The mouli produces a smooth, thick, pulpy mixture

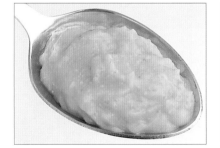

3 The finished puree has a smooth, uniform texture. It can be thinned out with a little of the water reserved from cooking, if necessary.

ORGANIC PRODUCE & PREPARING BABY FOODS

Growing demand has led to a greater variety of organic foods in the market. The use of pesticides and fertilizers is controlled by law, but there is as yet no firm evidence to show that foods grown without pesticides or artificial fertilizers are healthier. Organic farming is an environmentally friendly option, but it generates higher prices, and parents should not feel that a nonorganic diet is unhealthy. However, precautions can be taken: any residues in fresh produce are most likely to be in the skin, so remove any peel and discard the outer leaves of cabbage, lettuce, etc. If pesticides have been *absorbed* into the food, these measures will make no difference, but there is no evidence of any child being harmed by eating nonorganic produce.

Freezing & Reheating

COOKING IN BATCHES AND FREEZING is the most efficient and economical way to make food for your baby. Only a few purees – banana, avocado, melon, and eggplant, for example – do not freeze well. Food should be stored in a freezer that goes to 0°F (–18°C) or below in 24 hours. Food that has thawed should never be refrozen, although defrosted raw food may be cooked and then frozen again for later use.

Using frozen purees

1 Allow the freshly cooked puree to cool to room temperature, then spoon it into sterilized ice cube trays. Transfer the trays to the freezer.

2 When the puree has frozen solid, take the trays from the freezer and quickly push out the cubes onto a clean plate.

3 Set aside the required number of cubes and heat in a pan or microwave until piping hot all the way through (see below).

4 Transfer the remaining puree portions to a freezer bag, seal tightly, then label and date the contents. Return to the freezer.

Reheating rules

It is safe to thaw purees in a microwave or saucepan, as long as the food is then heated all the way through until piping hot. If using a microwave, be particularly careful since microwaves can heat food unevenly, producing "hot spots" but leaving other parts of the food cold. Let the puree cool after heating, and test the temperature before giving it to your baby. It can be dangerous to reheat food more than once, so reheat only one portion at a time to avoid unnecessary waste.

FREEZER STORAGE TIMES	
FOOD	TIME
Breast milk	1 month
Vegetable purees	6 months
Fruit purees	6 months
Purees with milk	2 months
Cooked fish dishes	3 months
Cooked meat dishes	3 months
Bread	2 months
Butter	6 months
Vegetables	6 months
Raw fish	3 months
Raw sausages	1 month
Other raw meat	3 months

Food Hygiene

BABIES AND YOUNG CHILDREN are especially vulnerable to the effects of food poisoning, so it is essential that great care is taken in the storage and preparation of their food. In the first few months of a baby's life, extra care must be taken (see below), but once your baby is mobile and exploring objects with his mouth, there is little point in sterilizing anything except bottles and nipples. Safe food handling, however, remains crucial.

Sterilizing equipment

Warm milk is a breeding ground for bacteria, so bottles must be scrupulously washed and sterilized. Sterilize all bottles, nipples, and training cup spouts up to age 1 year, and sterilize feeding spoons for the first 6 months. You can use an electric, steam, or microwave sterilizing kit, or simply boil feeding equipment in a pot of water for 10 minutes, or wash it in a dishwasher.

MICROWAVE STEAM STERILIZER

STERILIZING BY BOILING

General hygiene

Kitchen hygiene need not be complicated. Adhering to a few simple rules will minimize the likelihood of food contamination. You should always wash your hands before preparing food, and your child's hands should be washed before eating. Wipe daily with an antibacterial cleaner any surfaces that come into contact with your baby's food. Chopping boards and kitchen knives should be washed immediately after use, and equipment should be left to air-dry. Only clean dish towels should be used to dry your baby's dishes and utensils. Cover garbage cans and empty them frequently.

FOOD SAFETY TIPS

◆ KEEP RAW MEAT, FISH, AND EGGS away from other foods. Wash hands thoroughly after contact with any of these foods and use separate chopping boards for meat and fish and raw fruits and vegetables.

◆ ONLY REHEAT FOOD ONCE, and make sure it is reheated at a high temperature to kill off the bacteria.

◆ DO NOT KEEP your baby's half-eaten food for a later meal, because the saliva introduced from your baby's spoon will breed bacteria quickly.

◆ ALWAYS DATE FOOD stored in the freezer so that food that is past its prime, or that has even deteriorated and become harmful, is never eaten.

◆ DO NOT LEAVE FOOD unrefrigerated since bacteria multiply rapidly at room temperature; cool food quickly if it is to be refrigerated or frozen.

◆ COVER ALL FOOD AND DRINK securely to protect it against contamination by germ-carrying insects, and keep pets away from food and kitchen work surfaces.

4-6
Months

For your young baby, the first taste of
solids and the beginning of weaning is
a significant point in her development.
You may find that your baby takes to new
tastes and textures immediately, or you may
encounter a little initial wariness, but if
you attune yourself to your baby's individual
needs, this should be an enjoyable time of
learning and exploration for you both.

Starting solids

THE FIRST YEAR of life is a period of rapid growth and development, with most babies at least doubling their birth weight by the time they reach 6 months. For the first 6 months or so, breast milk or formula provides all the nutrients your baby needs, and indeed should be the main source of nourishment. However, at around 4 months she will reach a stage where she needs more concentrated sources of calories. Her first taste of solid food will be a significant milestone and mark the beginning of a gradual shift to a solid diet.

When does my baby need solids?

Don't be in a hurry to wean your baby onto solids because milk provides all the nutrients she needs in the first 6 months or so. Current medical advice is that solids should be withheld until at least 16 weeks after a baby's due date. A very young baby's digestive and immune systems are not sufficiently developed before this time and there is a higher risk of food allergy occurring (see page 11). Accordingly, if your baby was born prematurely, you may need to wait longer before beginning weaning. While sucking is a natural reflex, so too is gagging on unaccustomed solids. Babies have to be ready to learn the new skill of pushing food to the back of the mouth with their tongues and swallowing.

RECOGNIZING THE SIGNS

At around 16–20 weeks, your baby may show signs of being ready for her first taste of solids. She may no longer seem satisfied by her usual milk feedings and may become increasingly unsettled. If she has been sleeping through the night, she may start waking again to demand milk. She might also start showing interest in the things you eat.

TAKING THE
LEAD FROM YOUR BABY
Do not rush to introduce solids at the minimum recommended age. Look for signs from your baby that he is ready to try solids.

Foods for weaning

CHOOSING STARTER FOODS

Plain infant rice, mixed with expressed breast milk or formula, is a good starter food, but you can also introduce single-ingredient purees during the first 4 weeks of weaning. Simple purees enable you to assess how each new food has suited your child, and accustom her to a wide range of single fruits and vegetables before they are mixed together. Avoid any foods that might cause early allergies (see page 11). Root vegetables tend to be the most popular with young babies because of their naturally sweet flavor and smooth texture once pureed. Apples and pears are ideal first fruits, but taste them yourself before cooking since they must be ripe and sweet. Remember that infant rice is an excellent mixer too, since it can make strong-flavored foods more palatable to some babies. Alternatively, foods such as mashed banana, papaya, or avocado make nutritionally excellent no-cook purees.

WHY HOMEMADE IS BEST

If you make baby food yourself, you can be sure of using only the best ingredients, without the need for thickeners or additives. It is also more economical, and easier to establish a varied diet with food combinations designed to suit your baby. Homemade food has a fresher taste than commercial baby food, which may contain preservatives. Bought baby purees tend to be uniform and bland.

IDEAL FOODS

◆ APPLE ◆ PEAR ◆ PAPAYA ◆ BANANA ◆ AVOCADO ◆ BROCCOLI ◆ CARROT ◆ POTATO ◆ SWEET POTATO ◆ SQUASH OR PUMPKIN (SEE PAGES 26-7 FOR FURTHER INFORMATION).

REMEMBER

◆ ALWAYS WASH your hands thoroughly before preparing or offering food, and wash your baby's hands before feedings.

◆ FOR THINNING PUREES to the desired consistency of runny yogurt, use cooled boiled tap water, a little cooking water, or your baby's usual milk.

◆ DO NOT USE bottled mineral water since it is not sterile and also tends to have a high sodium content.

◆ FEEDING BOTTLES and spoons should be sterilized for the first 12 months, and bowls should be immersed in boiling water for 10 minutes or washed in a dishwasher (see page 19). Use a clean dish towel to dry utensils.

Getting started

Preparing tiny amounts of puree is time-consuming, so batch-cook and freeze portions, perhaps once a week (see page 18). Remember that at first your baby will only manage a "solid" consistency similar to runny yogurt, so the thickness of your prepared purees will change over the weeks. Alternatively, your baby's food can be prepared along with the rest of the family's: if you are cooking vegetables for your dinner, for example, simply cook without adding any seasoning, set aside a small portion for your baby, and puree it in a blender when she is ready for her meal.

SPECIAL EQUIPMENT

You will find suggestions for food preparation equipment on page 14. Your baby can take her first taste of solids from the tip of your finger, but once she is more accustomed to solids, you can use a small plastic weaning spoon and bowl. Plastic spoons have rounded edges that are kinder to tender gums. The spoon should be shallow too, so that your baby can easily suck the food from it. The bowl may have a handle that allows you to hold it up to your baby. Cover her clothes with a bib and have some wipes, or a damp cloth, on hand.

WEANING BOWL AND SPOON

Begin with 1 tablespoon of puree that is the consistency of runny yogurt.

Introducing your baby to solids

Pick a time of day for your baby's feeding when you are not rushed or likely to be distracted. If possible, choose the same time every day (perhaps lunchtime) so that you can begin to establish a routine. You may want to give your baby half her usual milk feeding before her solids so that she is not frantically hungry.

TESTING THE TEMPERATURE

Food should be room temperature or lukewarm. If using a microwave, heat the food until piping hot throughout, allow to cool, then stir well and check the temperature before feeding it to your baby.

JUDGING QUANTITIES

All babies' appetites and needs are different, but you will probably find that your baby initially takes 1–2 teaspoons of puree, so allow 1 tablespoon (15ml) or 1 ice cube portion. As she develops, offer a little more and continue until her interest starts to wane. When she has had enough of the solids, finish off with the second half of her milk feeding.

TAKING IT SLOWLY

Even though your baby may relish her solid food from the start, it will still take time for her to master the art of swallowing it. Let her enjoy her mealtimes by being relaxed yourself and taking things at your baby's pace. Avoid times when she is overtired or very restless. Talk to her encouragingly and make sure that she is comfortable, whether she is in a bouncy seat or cuddled on your lap. Show her that the experience is enjoyable by smiling and making eye contact and be prepared to get a little bit smeared with infant rice yourself.

THE FIRST
FEEDING EXPERIENCE
Your baby will probably
feel calm and reassured if you
choose a quiet time to begin her
food. Cradle her on your lap,
supporting her upper body and
head to make swallowing easy.

FIRST TASTES

Wash your hands thoroughly, then dip the tip of your finger into the food to test its temperature. If it is cool enough, let your baby suck the food from your finger to accustom her to the taste. The feel of your finger is probably familiar to her and lessens the strangeness of tasting "solids." You can then introduce a spoon. Have two on hand in case you drop one.

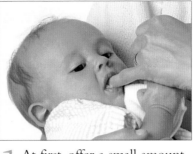

1 At first, offer a small amount of puree from the tip of your scrupulously clean finger and let her suck the food.

2 Coat the tip of a soft shallow weaning spoon with puree; don't overload it since this will make your baby splutter.

3 Place the spoon just between her lips, and let her suck the food off. If she spits the puree out, scrape it up and offer it again.

If your baby rejects food

Your baby may be one of the many who refuses solids at the first try. Be patient, it doesn't mean that she will never eat them. Wait and try again the next day. Initially, you are offering solids purely to introduce your baby to different foods. It is vital not to cut down on the amount of milk you give, since at this point solids are not replacing any part of her milk diet. If your baby seems to dislike a certain puree, try mixing it with a familiar or bland taste, such as breast milk, infant rice, or pureed potato, to make a gentler introduction. If

this does not work, simply stop offering that food and try again at a later date. Weaning is unlikely to take an uninterrupted course; there may be days when your baby refuses solids, perhaps if she is feeling sick or is in an unfamiliar environment, and wants only her comforting milk. Don't be anxious about this: a short break from solids will not harm your baby. Try reintroducing solid food after a few days, or prepare a runnier puree that is easier for your baby to swallow. At this early stage, as long as your baby is getting her

nutrition from milk, and as long as she continues to gain weight over a period of several days, she is probably getting enough food.

TAKING IT GENTLY
Follow your baby's lead during feeding. She may take a little time to become accustomed to solids, but increased familiarity will bring reassurance.

First Foods

VERY FIRST FOODS must be easy to digest and made of ingredients that will gently get your baby used to new flavors and textures. You may find that your baby immediately likes quite strong flavors, such as sweet potato, parsnip, or carrot, but some babies seem to prefer to begin with the more familiar tastes of milky infant rice or a bland potato puree. To begin with, purees should be quite runny and absolutely smooth, similar in consistency to runny yogurt, and made up of only one or two ingredients.

INFANT RICE

Specially formulated infant rice has a fine texture, is often fortified with minerals and iron, and can be mixed with cooled, boiled tap water, breast milk, or formula. It is easily digested and its milky taste makes an easy transition to solids. Choose a sugar-free variety, and cook according to package instructions.

POTATO PUREE

The mild taste of potato makes it a good weaning food for young babies. Use only baking potatoes and make the puree by pressing the mashed potato through a strainer. Do not use a food processor: it breaks down the starches and produces a sticky pulp. (See First Vegetable Puree on page 28.)

CARROT PUREE

Carrots, like many other root vegetables, blend well and have a naturally sweet taste that tends to appeal to babies. They should be steamed or boiled and blended with a spoonful of cooking water or your baby's usual milk to create a smooth-textured puree. (See First Vegetable Puree on page 28.)

BROCCOLI & POTATO PUREE

Broccoli is a good source of essential vitamins and can be blended to a smooth puree after brief steaming. However, babies may find its strong flavor distasteful, so it is best combined with strained boiled potato (see left) or infant rice to make a creamy puree. (See page 30 for recipe.)

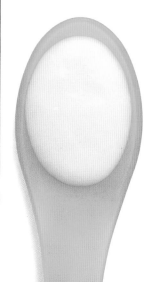 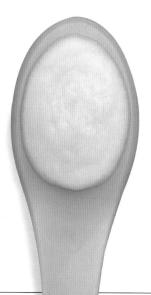  

SOME IDEAL FOODS

SMALL ZUCCHINI make a smooth puree that can be strained for young babies. Large zucchini may be unpleasantly bitter.

BUTTERNUT SQUASH is a good source of vitamin A. Although it can be steamed, its sweetness is enhanced by baking.

CANTALOUPE is the best source of vitamins A and C, but Galia melon tends to be sweeter than other melon varieties.

PARSNIP has a distinctly sweet taste that babies enjoy. It should be strained after pureeing to remove any traces of fiber.

ORANGE-FLESHED SWEET POTATO is an excellent source of beta-carotene and makes a sweet, soft, smooth puree.

PAPAYA needs no cooking if fully ripe. It can be pureed or mashed alone or with a little formula or breast milk added.

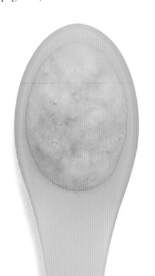
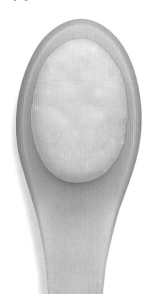

PEAR PUREE
Sweet ripe pear cooked in a little water until soft, then blended, makes an appealing first fruit puree for babies. Once your baby is 5 months old, there is no need to cook pears before pureeing, provided the fruit you choose is perfectly ripe and juicy.
(See First Fruit Puree on page 29.)

APPLE PUREE
Sweet eating apple varieties make a smooth applesauce. Once your baby has become accustomed to the taste, this puree can be mixed with other fruits. Try combining apple puree with a little infant rice or mild plain yogurt for a creamier finish.
(See First Fruit Puree on page 29.)

BANANA PUREE
A fully ripe banana makes an instant puree when thoroughly mashed. Its naturally sticky consistency can be modified by adding a little expressed breast milk or formula. Heating a banana in a microwave for a few seconds will make it easier to mash.
(See First Fruit Puree on page 29.)

INFANT RICE & DRIED APRICOT
Dried apricots are rich in beta-carotene and iron and useful when ripe summer fruits are scarce. Simmer soft, ready-to-eat apricots and press through a strainer to remove the skins. For an introduction to this fruit, puree with infant rice.
(See Dried Apricot Puree on page 31.)

FIRST VEGETABLE PUREE

½lb (250g) carrots or baking potatoes (or a mixture of the two), peeled

Your baby's first foods should be mild in taste, easy to digest, completely smooth, and unlikely to provoke an allergic reaction. Begin with single-ingredient purees in the first week or two, and then progress to combinations of root vegetables (see pages 22–25 for advice).

1 Chop the carrots or potatoes into small pieces. Put in a steamer or colander set over boiling water and cook for about 15 minutes, or until tender. Alternatively, place in a pot, pour in just enough boiling water to cover, and simmer, covered, for 15 minutes, or until soft.

2 Blend the vegetables to a puree using some of the liquid from the bottom of the steamer or the pot (see page 16).

3 Spoon a little puree into your baby's bowl and serve lukewarm. Pour the remainder into sterilized ice cube trays and freeze (see page 18).

VARIATION

Substitute other root vegetables, such as parsnip or rutabaga. Chop, cook, and blend as described above.

 Preparation/cooking
5 minutes/15 minutes

 Makes 8 portions

 Suitable for freezing

See page 26 for illustrations.

——— TIPS ———
The amount of liquid needed depends on whether your baby finds swallowing difficult. A general rule is to make an absolutely smooth, very runny puree, similar to runny yogurt.

Do not puree potato or sweet potato in a food processor because the mixture will become starchy and gluey. Use a mouli or sieve to puree potato.

CREAMY VEGETABLE PUREE

1 tbsp sugar-free, vitamin- and iron-enriched infant rice

3 tbsp formula or breast milk

4 tbsp first vegetable puree (see above)

Strong-tasting root vegetable purees, such as parsnip or carrot, may be made milder with the addition of infant rice. Infant rice also combines well with steamed and pureed broccoli and cauliflower.

1 Mix together the rice and milk, according to package instructions, and stir into the vegetable puree until thoroughly combined.

2 Spoon a little puree into your baby's bowl and serve lukewarm. Pour the remainder into sterilized ice cube trays and freeze (see page 18).

 Preparation/cooking
5 minutes/2 minutes

 Makes 6 portions

 Suitable for freezing

FIRST FRUIT PUREE

2 medium eating apples or
ripe pears, peeled and cored

1–2 tbsp water

Choose only sweet, completely ripe fruit for your baby. This will be a little thinner than a vegetable puree. Apple and pear puree mix together well.

1 Chop your chosen fruit into small, even-size pieces. Put the pieces into a heavy-bottomed saucepan with the water, cover, and cook over low heat until tender (about 10 minutes for apples, 4 minutes for pears).

2 Blend the fruit to a smooth puree using some of the cooking liquid, adding more cooled boiled water to thin it, if desired (see page 16).

3 Spoon a little puree into your baby's bowl and serve lukewarm. Pour the remainder into sterilized ice cube trays and freeze (see page 18).

VARIATION

Mash a raw banana or half a papaya and puree with approximately 2 tablespoons of breast milk or formula. If necessary, the banana can be heated in a microwave for a few seconds to make it easier to mash. These purees are not suitable for freezing.

 Preparation/cooking
5 minutes/5–10 minutes

 Makes 6 portions

 Suitable for freezing

See page 27 for illustrations.

— TIP —
All fruits for very first purees, except for banana, papaya, and avocado, must be cooked. At 5 months you can use raw peach, mango, plum, and melon, if they are ripe and juicy.

FRUITY INFANT RICE

1 tbsp sugar-free, vitamin-
and iron-enriched infant rice

3 tbsp formula or breast milk

4 tbsp first fruit puree
(see above)

Infant rice is a valuable first food: it is easily digested and has a milky taste that helps ease your baby's transition from a purely milk diet to solids. It may be served plain or combined with a puree.

1 Mix together the rice and milk, according to package instructions, and stir into the fruit puree to give it a slightly creamy texture.

2 Spoon a little puree into your baby's bowl and serve lukewarm. Pour the remainder into sterilized ice cube trays and freeze (see page 18).

 Preparation/cooking
5 minutes/2 minutes

 Makes 6 portions

 Suitable for freezing

SIMPLE VEGETABLE PUREES

*Denotes recipes that are not suitable for freezing.

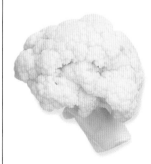

ZUCCHINI

BUTTERNUT SQUASH

CAULIFLOWER

ZUCCHINI

Zucchini can be used alone or mixed with carrot or potato puree (see First Vegetable Puree, page 28). Makes 8 servings.

Trim and slice ½lb (250g) zucchini. Place in a steamer and cook until tender, about 12 minutes. Alternatively, put in a pan with water to cover, bring to a boil, and simmer for 6 minutes. Blend to a puree, then strain, if desired.

BUTTERNUT SQUASH OR PUMPKIN

Squash are a good source of beta-carotene. Butternut squash combines well with pureed apple, pear, or peach (see First Fruit Puree, page 29). Makes 8 servings.

Peel and seed a 1lb (500g) squash or slice of pumpkin, then cut into small pieces. Cook as described for First Vegetable Puree on page 28, then blend to a puree, adding a little cooking water, if necessary. Alternatively, cut the squash in half, scoop out the seeds, and brush with melted butter. Cover with foil and bake in an oven preheated to 350°F/180°C for 1½ hours, or until tender.

SWEET POTATO

The orange-fleshed sweet potato is an excellent source of beta-carotene. It blends well with apple, pear, or peach puree (see First Fruit Puree, page 29). Makes 8 servings.

Scrub 10oz (300g) sweet potatoes, pat dry, and prick with a fork. Bake in an oven preheated to 400°F/200°C for 45 minutes–1 hour. Scoop out the flesh and mash together with 1–2 tablespoons of formula or breast milk. Alternatively, peel and cube the sweet potato and cook it as described for First Vegetable Puree on page 28.

CAULIFLOWER OR BROCCOLI

Cauliflower and broccoli have strong tastes and are best mixed with potato puree (see First Vegetable Puree, page 28) or infant rice. Makes 6 servings.

Place ½lb (250g) of small cauliflower or broccoli florets in a steamer and cook until tender, about 10 minutes. Drain and blend to a puree.

POTATO

SWEET POTATO

BROCCOLI

SIMPLE FRUIT PUREES

GALIA MELON

HONEYDEW MELON

MELON*

Melon makes a refreshing puree and combines well with mashed banana or avocado. Galia melons tend to be the sweetest variety. Makes 1 serving.

Take a small wedge of melon, remove the seeds, and cut the flesh away from the rind, discarding the greener flesh near the rind. Blend to a puree of the desired consistency.

PEACH OR NECTARINE*

Fresh, ripe peaches can be pureed on their own or mixed with infant rice, banana, or pear (see First Fruit Puree, page 29). They are suitable for babies over 5 months old. Makes 2 servings.

Score a cross on the base of a ripe peach or nectarine, then submerge in boiling water for 1 minute. Peel and chop the peach flesh, then puree in a blender. (Ripe, sweet peaches, nectarines, plums, and mangoes can be used raw.)

NECTARINE

DRIED APRICOTS

DRIED APRICOT

Dried, ready-to-eat apricots are rich in nutrients and useful when seasonal fruits are scarce. This is good mixed with infant rice or apple or pear puree (see First Fruit Puree, page 29). Makes 4 servings.

Simmer a handful of apricots in a little water for about 10 minutes, or until tender. Puree in a blender to the desired consistency, using as much of the cooking liquid as needed to make a smooth pulp. Work the pulp through a food mill or strong-meshed strainer to remove the fibrous skins.

AVOCADO

PAPAYA

AVOCADO*

Avocado is very nutritious and has a buttery flavor and texture that is generally popular with babies. It combines well with papaya, pear, or banana. Choose a soft ripe one and prepare just before your baby is ready to eat (to avoid discoloration). Makes 1 serving.

Halve the avocado, scoop out the pit, and mash half the flesh with a fork, or puree to the desired consistency with about 2 tablespoons of breast milk or formula.

6-9
Months

Once your baby has become accustomed to simple purees, he will be ready for more adventurous combinations of foods. Purees with stronger flavors and thicker textures can be introduced, along with simple finger foods that enable him to practice self-feeding. He will be growing rapidly, and his diet should be gradually adapted to reflect his changing needs.

Exploring Tastes

BETWEEN 6 AND 9 MONTHS is a time of rapid development, and your baby will spend many more hours awake than previously. It is a good idea to introduce plenty of new flavors, in addition to the ones he already knows. Since everything is new for him, he will be receptive to these changes. This is a stage when solids should become a fixed part of your baby's daily diet.

Moving on from purees

LEARNING TO CHEW

Every baby develops at his own pace, but your baby's first tooth (a front incisor) will probably be cut at around 6–7 months; the remaining incisors usually follow in the next 5 months. As teeth begin to emerge, you can introduce coarser textures. Your baby will mostly use his gums to chew, so mashed and finely chopped food will provide ample chewing practice. It is not a good idea to offer smooth purees for too long since your baby may become lazy about chewing and have difficulty developing the tongue movements needed to deal with real solids. If he refuses lumpy food, make the transition easier by introducing a little mashed or grated food into his usual purees, or perhaps make a favorite meal in a thicker or coarser form. Introduce wider combinations of ingredients and don't be afraid to mix sweet with savory: fruit combined with vegetables, fish, or meat often appeals to babies.

INTRODUCING COW'S MILK

You can now use cow's milk in cooking and with breakfast cereals, but formula or breast milk should remain your baby's main drink since these contain nutrients that cow's milk lacks, such as iron and vitamin D. Iron is particularly vital. Babies are born with sufficient iron reserves for the first 6 months of life, but after that, iron is required from food sources. Follow-up milks, which contain more iron than standard formulas, are designed for babies between 4 months and 2 years. Because they are more difficult to digest than ordinary formula milk, they should not be given to babies under 4 months. Up to the age of 1 year, babies should have at least ⅔ pint (400ml) of milk each day, mostly in the form of their usual breast milk or formula. Obviously this is difficult to measure precisely, especially if you are still breast-feeding. However, a portion of milk intake can come from dairy foods such as yogurt or cheese. If you are breast-feeding, your baby will be receiving plenty of thirst-quenching foremilk (the first milk in any breast-feeding). Formula-fed babies will probably need small amounts of cooled boiled water to drink as well as their usual milk, because formula is a little less thirst-quenching than breast milk.

CHEWING PRACTICE
A finger of oven-baked whole wheat toast makes a good teething rusk.

NEW FOODS FOR YOUR BABY

BREAD AND CEREALS, including whole wheat bread, rusks, whole grain low-sugar breakfast cereals (mini wheat crackers and hot oatmeal) can now be given. Avoid large amounts of high-fiber foods, such as high-fiber bread or bran flakes – these are too difficult for young babies to digest.

DAIRY PRODUCTS, such as pasteurized regular yogurt and fromage frais; cottage cheese, cream cheese, and mild hard cheeses, such as Cheddar and Edam, are excellent nutrient-rich foods. Low-fat foods, such as reduced-fat spreads, are not suitable since they are too low in calories for a growing baby.

EGGS, if hard-boiled, and dishes made of well-cooked eggs, such as eggy fried bread, omelets, frittatas, or scrambled eggs, are fast to cook and nutritious. Do not serve raw or lightly cooked eggs (there is some risk of salmonella). The white and yolk should be cooked through until solid.

FISH FILLETS, such as flounder, cod, whiting, or salmon, may be made into a puree with potato and zucchini, or perhaps blended with homemade cheese sauce. Canned sardines are useful sources of iron and essential fatty acids. Check all fish carefully for bones before serving.

RED MEAT, for example, lean ground beef or lamb, can be combined with sautéed onion, potato, and mushrooms, then finely chopped in a blender. Liver, which is easily digested, provides the best source of iron. Slow-cooked lamb, pork, or beef casseroles make good purees.

CHICKEN is generally popular with babies because of its mild taste. Serve it chopped or pureed, in a casserole or poached. It combines well with root vegetables like potato and carrot, and with fruits such as apple, grapes, mango, or papaya.

VEGETABLES, including onions, leeks, cabbage, kale, green beans, spinach, and other leafy green vegetables, red peppers, tomatoes, corn, peas, and mushrooms, greatly expand the dietary repertoire. Frozen vegetables often keep as many nutrients as fresh ones.

FRUITS, particularly mangoes, grapes (peeled, seeded, and halved), citrus fruits and berries, can be served. Remove the pith from citrus fruits and strain out seeds from berries. Use berries in small quantities as they can be indigestible. (Some babies have a strawberry allergy.)

BEANS AND LEGUMES are ideal for boosting meat purees, but they are especially valuable for vegetarian babies. Lentils and dried legumes (such as split peas or lima beans) are a good source of protein and iron. Tofu (soybean curd) is a good meat alternative.

Family meals with your baby

Once your baby can support his head and upper body, you can introduce him to a high chair. As long as his back is supported, he will feel comfortable and he will enjoy being higher up and able to see what is going on around him. Put him in a safety strap so that he can't topple out, pull the chair away from the wall, and put a plastic mat on the floor to make cleaning up easier. Let him get used to being in the chair, wearing a bib, and having a tray in front of him by giving him the chance to play there with his favorite toys. When you feed him, give him his own plastic spoon to hold. If he drinks milk from a bottle, let him have that in the high chair at first. He will soon be ready to enjoy eating there.

FIRST REFUSALS

If he finds it strange at first to be fed in this new way, he may even reject the food, turning his head away each time. Don't be put off by his initial refusal. Gently encourage him to feed himself, even though it is a messy business. His hand-to-eye coordination will be improving all the time and he'll soon start dipping his spoon in and out of the food and aiming it at his mouth.

JOINING IN

Even though your baby has only just begun to take solids and has many more meals than older members of the family, draw his high chair up to the table so that he can join you at meals whenever possible. He will learn that meals are sociable and fun as well as satisfying for his stomach. Try to plan and vary his menus along the lines of the family mealtimes. For example, give him infant rice or cereal for breakfast, a savory dish followed by pieces of fruit or cheese for lunch, and perhaps a selection of finger foods with his milk for dinner.

EATING TOGETHER
Your baby will now be taking 2–3 tablespoons of solid food at mealtimes. You'll need to help her get most of the food to the right destination, but encourage her attempts at feeding herself.

DRINKS AT MEALTIMES

Now that solid food is beginning to replace part of your baby's milk diet at mealtimes, he will need to start drinking water to quench his thirst. It is best to start with sterile cooled boiled water rather than water straight from the tap and to avoid sweetened fruit juices or herbal drinks. Drinks with added sugar or artificial sweeteners are too sugary for babies or toddlers, and tea or coffee shouldn't be given since they reduce iron absorption and are stimulants. On the other hand, diluted orange juice is a useful source of vitamin C and can be given from time to time. Now is the moment to introduce a training cup. These have lids in various designs, but your baby may prefer one that allows him to use the familiar sucking mechanism. Cups with soft, flexible spouts can eventually be replaced by cups with shorter, firmer spouts, perhaps at around 8–9 months. He will still be getting most of his liquid from his usual milk and some from the purees he eats, but a cup of water that he can handle by himself at the table will allow him to choose when he wants to drink and how much.

Vegetarian meals

Parents who follow a vegetarian diet sometimes worry that this may not be suitable for their children. It is true that a bulky, high-fiber vegetarian diet is not suitable for growing young children because it is too low in calories and essential fats, and even hinders absorption of iron. However, a vegetarian diet is perfectly adequate for babies and small children as long as meals are carefully balanced. Animal proteins, including those found in egg and dairy products, are high quality with essential amino acids. Vegetable proteins, as in beans, legumes, and seeds, provide a lower quality protein and should be eaten in combination with each other or with small quantities of egg or dairy foods to provide a complete protein; for example, a lentil puree with grated cheese. You can introduce legumes such as beans or lentils, soy products, and cheese at around 6 months, although babies will not need the additional protein supplied by these foods until at least 9 months because breast milk or formula provides enough for their needs. The vegetarian diet is sometimes low in iron, but vitamin C-rich products, such as diluted orange juice, greatly increase the absorption of iron from nonanimal iron sources so you can gradually introduce juice as a drink at mealtimes. If you intend to follow a vegan weaning plan (i.e., without dairy products or eggs), you should plan your child's diet carefully, in consultation with a doctor or pediatric nutritionist.

REMEMBER

♦ NEVER LEAVE YOUR BABY alone when he is eating. If he is in a high chair, always use a strap that goes around his body and clips on to the chair.

♦ NEVER FORCE YOUR BABY to eat a food he does not want or to finish a meal. Let your baby's appetite be your guide.

♦ ALLOW YOUR BABY to practice feeding himself. This will be messy, so position him away from the walls and put a mat or an old plastic tablecloth under his chair to make cleaning easier.

♦ EAT WITH YOUR BABY whenever possible. Try to make feeding a sociable experience from the start.

♦ DON'T GIVE CHILDREN tea or coffee since they hinder iron absorption. High-fiber cereals also interfere with iron absorption.

VEGETARIAN FINGER FOODS
When your baby begins to grasp objects, finger foods in the form of steamed vegetables, ripe fruit, or cheese shapes become a useful part of her diet.

New Tastes & Textures

ONCE YOUR BABY HAS ADJUSTED TO SIMPLE PUREES, you can begin to introduce a broader range of flavors and textures. If he has become adept at chewing, he is now ready for basic finger foods, and you should gradually introduce purees with thicker or lumpier textures. You can also combine more ingredients to make interesting flavors. Don't be afraid to mix sweet with savory: fruit with pureed chicken or fish, for example, is a favorite with many babies.

SMOOTH TEXTURES

The introduction of thicker mixtures should be gradual, beginning with familiar flavors blended with new ingredients. Keep textures smooth until your baby can cope well with chewing and swallowing.

PEACH, APPLE & STRAWBERRY PUREE

Make this puree when peaches are in season and soft fruit is ripe and sweet. It can be mixed with infant rice for a milder taste. (See page 41 for recipe.)

PAPAYA & COTTAGE CHEESE

Creamy cottage cheese is blended with juicy papaya to make a fruity, nutritious, no-cook meal. (See page 40 for recipe.)

POTATO, LEEK & PEA PUREE

This combination of vegetables blended with unsalted fresh stock makes a mild-tasting puree. (See page 42 for recipe.)

FOODS FOR CHEWING PRACTICE

Babies may not derive much nutritional benefit from finger foods at this stage, but these foods will give valuable chewing and biting practice. Your baby will also enjoy trying to hold foods by himself: offer him whole wheat toast strips, hard, mild cheese cut into easily grasped pieces, and low-sugar rusks.

MILD CHEESE

RUSK COOKIES

WHOLE WHEAT TOAST

NEW TEXTURES

As new teeth emerge, introduce mashed or finely chopped food to accustom your baby to chewing. Try adding just a little grated or mashed food to a smooth puree, or make his favorite puree in a lumpier form.

TOMATO & CAULIFLOWER GRATIN

This blended gratin makes a good introduction to cauliflower. Cheddar cheese and seeded tomatoes boost the flavor. (See page 44 for recipe.)

FISH WITH CARROTS & ORANGE

This puree made with fresh white fish is bursting with needed nutrients. (See page 46 for recipe.)

FIRST CHICKEN CASSEROLE

Tender chicken breast paired with sweet root vegetables is usually popular with babies. (See page 47 for recipe.)

INSTANT NO-COOK PUREES

*Denotes recipes that are not suitable for freezing.

There are many fast, no-cook purees that are both delicious and nutritious for your baby. Below are some good fruit combinations to try. Each makes 1 portion.

TIP

Always make sure that any raw fruit you give to your baby is fully ripened and sweet.

BANANA

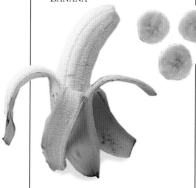

PAPAYA

PLUMS

AVOCADO & PAPAYA PUREE

BANANA & PEACH*

Peel and pit a small ripe peach (see page 31), then puree or mash half the flesh with half a small ripe banana. Rich source of fiber, folic acid, and vitamin C.

PAPAYA & COTTAGE CHEESE OR YOGURT*

Cut a small ripe papaya in half, remove the black seeds, and puree or mash the flesh of one of the halves with 1 tablespoon of sieved cottage cheese or plain yogurt. See page 38 for illustration. Rich source of beta-carotene, protein, vitamin B12, and vitamin C.

AVOCADO & BANANA OR PAPAYA*

Mash a quarter of a small avocado together with half a small ripe banana and 1–2 tablespoons of milk. You can substitute the flesh of half a papaya for the banana in this recipe – the milk is then optional. Rich source of fiber, folic acid, vitamin B12, vitamin C, and vitamin E.

PLUM OR APRICOT & PEAR

Peel and pit a ripe apricot or plum. Slice the fruit and puree or mash the flesh with a peeled, cored, and chopped soft ripe pear. Rich source of fiber and vitamin C.

MANGO & BANANA*

Puree or mash the flesh of a quarter of a small mango with half a small ripe banana. Rich source of beta-carotene and vitamin C.

PAPAYA & CHICKEN

Cut a small ripe papaya in half, remove the black seeds, and puree or mash the flesh of one of the halves with 1oz (30g) cooked boneless chicken. Rich source of beta-carotene, fiber, protein, and B vitamins.

PEACH

AVOCADO

PEAR

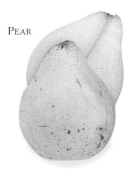

PLUM & PEAR PUREE

APRICOT, PEAR, PEACH & APPLE COMPOTE

3 ready-to-eat dried apricots or fresh apricots

1 eating apple, peeled, cored, and chopped

1 large ripe pear, peeled, cored, and chopped

1 large ripe peach or plum, peeled, pitted, and chopped

For a creamier finish, mix 2 tablespoons of infant rice with 4 tablespoons of milk and blend this with the fruit puree.

Simmer the fruit in a saucepan with a little water until soft, 8–10 minutes, then blend to a puree of the desired consistency.

 Preparation/cooking
5 minutes/10 minutes

 Makes 4 portions

 Nutritional information
Rich source of fiber and vitamin C.

 Suitable for freezing

APPLE, KIWI & PEAR PUREE

1 eating apple, peeled, cored, and chopped

3 tbsp pure apple juice

1 ripe pear, peeled, cored, and chopped

1 ripe kiwi, peeled and chopped

2 tbsp infant rice

Infant rice enables you to produce a good puree consistency and makes a suitable base for new flavors. Here it is mixed with vitamin-rich kiwi.

1 Put the apple in a pan with the apple juice. Cover and simmer gently for about 8 minutes. Add the pear and kiwi and continue to simmer the fruit for 3–4 minutes.

2 Blend the fruit to a puree and strain to get rid of the kiwi's black seeds. Stir in the rice (no need to cook) while the puree is warm.

 Preparation/cooking
5 minutes/12 minutes

 Makes 4 portions

 Nutritional information
Rich source of fiber and vitamin C.

 Suitable for freezing

PEACH, APPLE & STRAWBERRY PUREE

1 eating apple, peeled, cored, and chopped

1 large ripe peach, peeled, pitted, and chopped

3 large strawberries

—— NOTE ——
Strawberries occasionally provoke an allergic reaction in sensitive babies.

This is a delicious fruit puree to make in the summer. It can be combined with some infant rice mixed with a little milk or water.

Steam the apple for about 6 minutes, or until tender. Add the peach and strawberries to the steamer, and continue to cook for about 3 minutes. Blend the fruits to a smooth puree.

 Preparation/cooking
5 minutes/12 minutes

 Makes 4 portions

 Nutritional information
Rich source of fiber and vitamin C.

 Suitable for freezing

See page 38 for illustration.

JUICY PEAR & PRUNE PUREE

2 ripe pears, peeled, cored, and chopped

2 pitted prunes, chopped

1 tbsp infant rice

This tasty combination of fresh and dried fruits is a useful source of fiber.

Simmer the fruit in a saucepan with a little water for 5 minutes. Puree to the desired consistency, using as much cooking water as needed. Strain to get rid of the tough prune skins. Stir in the infant rice while warm.

 Preparation/cooking
5 minutes/5 minutes

 Makes 2 portions

 Nutritional information
Rich source of fiber and vitamin C.

 Suitable for freezing

DRIED APRICOTS WITH SEMOLINA

¼ cup (60g) ready-to-eat dried apricots

1½ tbsp semolina

¾ cup (175ml) milk

Dried apricots blend very well with semolina, and they are a concentrated source of nutrients. This puree makes an excellent breakfast.

1 Put the apricots in a small saucepan and just cover them with water. Bring to a boil, then reduce the heat and simmer for about 8 minutes, or until the apricots are tender (add a little more water, if necessary).

2 Put the semolina in a saucepan and gradually stir in the milk over medium heat. Bring to a boil and stir for about 3 minutes, or until thickened. Combine the apricots with the semolina and blend to a puree of the desired consistency.

NOTE
Semolina is a wheat product and should not be given to babies with actual or suspected gluten intolerance.

Cooking
12 minutes

Makes 4 portions

Nutritional information
Rich source of beta-carotene, fiber, and vitamin B12.

Suitable for freezing

TIP
If using frozen portions, it may be necessary to add extra milk once the puree is defrosted to thin the consistency.

BUTTERNUT SQUASH & APPLE

1lb (500g) butternut squash or pumpkin, peeled, seeded, and chopped

1 eating apple, peeled, cored, and chopped

Mixing vegetables with fruit is a good way to encourage babies to eat vegetables. Apple brings out the natural sweetness of butternut squash.

Put the butternut squash in a steamer and cook for about 7 minutes. Add the apple to the steamer and continue to cook for about 10 minutes, or until the squash is tender. Blend to a smooth puree.

VARIATION
Omit the apple and blend the cooked squash or pumpkin with a large, juicy, peeled raw peach.

Preparation/cooking
5 minutes/17 minutes

Makes 4 portions

Nutritional information
Rich source of beta-carotene, fiber, folic acid, and vitamin C.

Suitable for freezing

POTATO, LEEK & PEA PUREE

2 tbsp (30g) butter

1 leek, white part only, washed and sliced

1 large potato, peeled and chopped

1 cup (250ml) unsalted chicken stock (see page 46) or water

½ cup (60g) frozen peas

Use only unsalted stock for this recipe, canned or homemade. To make this puree into a delicious soup for the family, simply add extra stock and seasoning.

1 Heat the butter in a pan, add the leek, and sauté until just golden, 5–6 minutes. Add the potato and pour in the stock. Bring to a boil, then reduce the heat, cover, and simmer for 10 minutes.

2 Add the frozen peas and continue to cook for about 6 minutes, or until the vegetables are tender. Blend to a puree using a mouli or strainer.

Preparation/cooking
5 minutes/24 minutes

Makes 4 portions

Nutritional information
Rich source of fiber, folic acid, vitamin A, and vitamin C.

Suitable for freezing

See page 38 for illustration.

TRIO OF ROOT VEGETABLES

1 cup (175g) chopped carrots

1 large potato, peeled and chopped

1¼ cups (125g) peeled and chopped parsnips or rutabaga

—— TIP ——
Use a mouli or strainer to make this puree; a food processor makes cooked potato gluey.

Babies tend to love root vegetables because of their naturally sweet flavor.

1 Put the vegetables in a saucepan and just cover with boiling water. Cook over medium heat for about 20 minutes, or until tender. Alternatively, steam them until tender.

2 Blend the vegetables to a smooth puree with about ½ cup (125ml) of the cooking liquid or use boiled water from the bottom of the steamer.

 Preparation/cooking
5 minutes/21 minutes

 Makes 6 portions

 Nutritional information
Rich source of beta-carotene, fiber, folic acid, and vitamin C.

Suitable for freezing

LENTIL & VEGETABLE PUREE

2 tbsp (30g) butter

¼lb (125g) leeks, finely sliced

2 tbsp (30g) chopped celery

1 cup (125g) peeled and chopped carrots

½ cup (60g) red lentils

½lb (250g) sweet potatoes, peeled and chopped

1 bay leaf

2 cups (475ml) unsalted chicken stock (see page 46) or water

Lentils are a good source of protein. However, some babies find lentils indigestible, so it is best not to give them before 8 months.

1 Melt the butter in a saucepan, add the leeks, and sauté for 2–3 minutes. Stir in the celery, carrots, and lentils and cook for 2 more minutes.

2 Add the sweet potatoes and bay leaf and cover with the stock or water. Bring to a boil, then reduce the heat, cover, and simmer for about 30 minutes, or until the vegetables and lentils are tender. Remove the bay leaf. Blend to a puree for young babies. Older babies can eat it as is.

 Preparation/cooking
10 minutes/40 minutes

 Makes 8 portions

 Nutritional information
Rich source of beta-carotene, fiber, folic acid, protein, and vitamin C.

 Suitable for freezing

SPINACH, POTATO, PARSNIP & LEEK

2 tbsp (30g) butter

1 leek, white part only, thinly sliced

½lb (250g) potatoes, chopped

¼lb (125g) parsnips, chopped

1¼ cups (300ml) boiling water

¼lb (125g) fresh spinach, washed, with tough stalks removed, or 2oz (60g) frozen spinach

1 Melt the butter in a saucepan, add the leek, and sauté for 2–3 minutes. Add the potatoes and parsnips, sauté for 1 minute, then cover with the boiling water. Cover and simmer for 20 minutes.

2 Add the fresh spinach leaves, if using, and continue to cook for 3–4 minutes. If using frozen spinach, cook it in a microwave or saucepan according to package instructions, then squeeze out the excess water. Add the spinach to the potato, leek, and parsnip mixture and cook for about 2 minutes.

3 Blend the vegetables to a puree of the desired consistency, adding more water to thin the puree if needed.

 Preparation/cooking
10 minutes/30 minutes

 Makes 6 portions

 Nutritional information
Rich source of beta-carotene, fiber, folic acid, and vitamin C.

 Suitable for freezing

SWEET POTATO, CARROT & BROCCOLI

2 medium sweet potatoes, peeled and chopped

1 large carrot, sliced

½ cup (125g) broccoli florets

It can be a good idea to combine popular vegetables with varieties that children tend to like a little less. In this recipe, I have used carrot and sweet potato, which babies usually love to eat, to tone down the strong flavor of broccoli.

1 Put the sweet potatoes and carrot in a steamer and cook for 10 minutes. Add the broccoli and continue to cook for about 7 minutes, or until all the vegetables are tender.

2 Blend the vegetables with 6–7 tablespoons of water from the bottom of the steamer to make a puree of the desired consistency.

 Preparation/cooking
5 minutes/18 minutes

 Makes 6 portions

 Nutritional information
Rich source of beta-carotene, fiber, folic acid, and vitamin C.

 Suitable for freezing

TOMATO & CAULIFLOWER GRATIN

2 cups (150g) cauliflower florets

2 tbsp (30g) butter

½lb (250g) tomatoes, peeled, seeded, and roughly chopped

¼ cup (30g) grated Cheddar cheese

1 Put the cauliflower florets in a steamer and cook until soft, about 12 minutes.

2 Meanwhile, melt the butter in a pan, add the tomatoes and sauté until mushy. Remove from the heat and add the cheese, stirring until melted. Mix the cauliflower with the tomato and cheese sauce, then blend to the desired consistency.

VARIATION

Steam the cauliflower until soft, then blend with 3 tablespoons of cheese sauce (see page 71 for recipe), omitting the seasoning from the sauce.

 Preparation/cooking
5 minutes/20 minutes

 Makes 4 portions

 Nutritional information
Rich source of beta-carotene, folic acid, protein, vitamin B12, and vitamin C.

 Suitable for freezing

See page 39 for illustration.

FILLET OF COD WITH A TRIO OF VEGETABLES

¼lb (125g) potatoes, peeled and chopped

1 cup (125g) sliced carrots

¼lb (125g) cod fillet, skinned

3 peppercorns, 1 bay leaf, and a sprig of parsley

½ cup (100ml) milk

1 tbsp (15g) butter

1 tomato, peeled, seeded, and chopped

This dish has a fairly mild taste and, because the proportion of fish to vegetables is quite small, it makes a gentle introduction to fish for your baby.

1 Put the vegetables in a saucepan and cover with water. Bring to a boil, then reduce the heat, cover, and cook for 20 minutes, or until tender.

2 Meanwhile, put the fish in a pan with the peppercorns, bay leaf, and parsley. Cover with the milk, then poach the fish for about 5 minutes, or until it flakes easily. Strain the milk from the fish and reserve. Discard the herbs.

3 Melt the butter in a pan, add the tomato, and sauté until mushy. Flake the fish with a fork, checking carefully for bones. Drain the vegetables, then add them to the fish with the tomato and ¼ cup (60ml) of the reserved milk. Blend to a puree of the desired consistency.

  Preparation/cooking
10 minutes/25 minutes

 Makes 4 portions

 Nutritional information
Rich source of beta-carotene, folic acid, protein, vitamin B12, and vitamin C.

Suitable for freezing

FLOUNDER FILLET WITH LEEK & CHEESE SAUCE

5oz (150g) flounder fillet, skinned

3 peppercorns, 1 bay leaf, and a sprig of parsley

¾ cup (175ml) milk

2 tbsp (30g) butter

¼ cup (60g) finely chopped leek

1 tbsp flour

¼ cup (45g) grated Cheddar or Edam cheese

Another good way to introduce fish to your baby is to mix it with cheese sauce. Use spinach or zucchini instead of leek if you prefer.

1 Put the fish in a pan with the peppercorns, herbs, and milk. Bring to a boil, then simmer, covered, for 5 minutes, or until the fish flakes easily. Strain the milk and reserve. Discard the herbs. Flake the fish with a fork, checking for bones.

2 Meanwhile, melt the butter in a saucepan, add the leek, and sauté until softened.

3 Stir the flour into the leek mixture to make a paste and cook for 1 minute. Gradually add the reserved milk, bring to a boil, and cook, stirring, until thickened. Remove the sauce from the heat and add the cheese, stirring until melted. Puree the fish with the leek and cheese sauce.

  Preparation/cooking
5 minutes/15 minutes

 Makes 4 portions

 Nutritional information
Rich source of calcium, folic acid, protein, vitamin A, vitamin B6, and vitamin B12.

Suitable for freezing

FISH WITH CARROTS & ORANGE

This puree is rich in vitamins and calcium, and bursting with flavor. Flounder is an excellent fish to choose for young babies since it has a very soft texture.

1¼ cups (175g) scraped and sliced carrots

¼lb (125g) potatoes, peeled and chopped

6oz (175g) flounder fillets

juice of 1 orange

2oz (60g) grated mild Cheddar cheese

1 tbsp (15g) butter

1 Put the vegetables in a pan, cover with water, and boil until soft. Alternatively, place them in a steamer and cook until tender.

2 Meanwhile, place the fish in a gratin dish, cover with the orange juice, scatter the cheese, and dot with butter. Cover, leaving an air vent, and microwave on high for 3 minutes, or until the fish flakes easily. Alternatively, cover with foil and cook in the preheated oven for about 20 minutes.

3 Flake the fish with a fork, checking for bones. Add the vegetables to the fish and its juices, then blend to a puree of the desired consistency.

 Preparation/cooking
5 minutes/20 minutes

 Oven temperature
microwave on high or conventional oven at 350°F/180°C

 Makes 6 portions

 Nutritional information
Rich source of beta-carotene, calcium, folic acid, protein, vitamin B6, and vitamin B12.

 Suitable for freezing

See page 39 for illustration.

GRANDMA'S CHICKEN SOUP & STOCK

I use fresh chicken stock as the base for many of my recipes. This makes a delicious soup for older family members if it is fortified with tiny soup pasta or vermicelli and enriched with bouillon cubes.

1 large chicken with giblets, cut into 8 pieces and trimmed of excess fat, or 1 roast chicken carcass, broken up

12 cups (2.5 liters) water

2 large onions, roughly chopped

3 large carrots, roughly sliced

2 parsnips, roughly chopped

2 leeks, sliced

1 celery stalk

2 parsley sprigs

2 or 3 chicken bouillon cubes (for babies over 1 year)

1 Put the raw or cooked chicken pieces into a very large pot and cover with water. Slowly bring to a boil and skim off any scum that comes to the surface.

2 Add all the remaining ingredients, including the bouillon cubes, if making it for older children. Cover and simmer gently for about 2 hours, checking occasionally and adding more water as necessary. Remove the chicken pieces. If you have used a whole chicken, strip off the flesh and set aside. Return the bones to the pot and cook for another hour.

3 Remove the pot from the heat and allow to cool. Chill for at least 4 hours or overnight, then skim off the layer of fat from the surface.

4 Strain the stock through a sieve into a clean pot or bowl. If desired, you can make a puree by blending a little of the stock together with some of the cooked vegetables and pieces of chicken.

 Preparation/cooking
10 minutes plus 4 hours refrigeration/2 hours

 Makes 7½ cups (1.85 liters)

 Suitable for freezing

— TIP —
As a shortcut, make your own stock from the leftover carcass of a roast chicken, adding giblets, if available, and perhaps a veal marrow bone from the butcher for extra flavor.

— NOTE —
Do not use bouillon cubes in food for babies under 1 year because they contain large amounts of salt.

FIRST CHICKEN CASSEROLE

1 tbsp vegetable oil

¼ cup (100g) carrots, chopped

¼ cup (60g) sliced leeks, white part only

2½oz (75g) chicken breast, cut into chunks

½lb (250g) potatoes, peeled and chopped

½ cup (75g) peeled and chopped parsnips

boiling water

Babies tend to like the mild taste of chicken. Here I have combined it with vegetables that have a naturally sweet taste. Root vegetables are also good since they help give a smooth texture.

1 Heat the oil in a pan, add the carrots and leeks, and sauté until softened, about 6 minutes. Add the chicken and sauté, turning occasionally, until seared, but not browned.

2 Add the potatoes and parsnips and just cover with boiling water. Cover and simmer for about 15 minutes, or until everything is tender and cooked through. Blend to a puree, or leave chopped for older babies.

 Preparation/cooking
10 minutes/22 minutes

 Makes 6 portions

 Nutritional information
Rich source of beta-carotene, folic acid, protein, and vitamin A.

 Suitable for freezing

See page 39 for illustration.

TASTY GROUND MEAT WITH RUTABAGA & TOMATO

½ tbsp vegetable oil

2 tbsp finely chopped onion

¼lb (125g) lean ground beef

¼lb (125g) organic chicken livers (optional)

½lb (250g) rutabaga, chopped

2 tomatoes, peeled, seeded, and chopped

1 cup (250ml) unsalted chicken stock (see page 46) or beef stock

This makes a good introduction to ground meat. It has a nice soft texture and a natural sweetness provided by the rutabaga.

1 Heat the oil in a skillet, add the onion, and sauté until softened. Add the ground beef and chicken livers, if using, and sauté, stirring occasionally, until browned.

2 Add the rutabaga and tomatoes, cover with the stock, using less if a thicker consistency is preferred, and bring to a boil. Reduce the heat, cover, and cook for 30 minutes. Blend to a puree of the desired consistency.

 Preparation/cooking
10 minutes/40 minutes

 Makes 8 portions

 Nutritional information
Rich source of folic acid, protein, vitamin B12, and zinc.

 Suitable for freezing

BRAISED BEEF WITH CARROT, PARSNIP & POTATO

2 tbsp (30g) butter

1 cup (125g) leeks, sliced

6oz (175g) lean stewing beef, cut into cubes

1¼ cups (150g) sliced carrots

1 cup (125g) peeled and chopped parsnips

½lb (250g) potatoes, chopped

2 cups (450ml) unsalted beef stock or chicken stock (see opposite)

This combination of root vegetables and beef has a smooth consistency that appeals to young babies.

1 Heat the butter in a flameproof casserole, add the leeks, and sauté for 5 minutes, or until softened. Add the beef and sauté until browned.

2 Add the carrots, parsnips, and potatoes to the casserole, cover with the stock, and bring the mixture to a boil.

3 Transfer the casserole to the preheated oven and cook for 1½–2 hours, or until the meat is soft. Blend to a puree of the desired consistency.

 Preparation/cooking
10 minutes/1¾–2¼ hours

 Oven temperature
350°F/180°C

 Makes 10 portions

 Nutritional information
Rich source of beta-carotene, folic acid, niacin, protein, vitamin B1, vitamin B12, and zinc.

 Suitable for freezing

9-12
Months

Solid foods should now be the
focus of your child's meals. This is a
time of growing independence and your
baby may insist on feeding herself. She will
probably be much more proficient at
chewing now, and chopped or mashed food
can replace purees. Foods from previous
chapters can still be served to her; simply
adjust the texture, as necessary.

Growing Appetites

AS SHE APPROACHES her first birthday, your baby will experience a broader range of foods, and she will have started to transfer her allegiance from milk to "grown-up" meals. Her increasing sense of autonomy will show itself in her change from a passive eater to an active eater as she enjoys trying to feed herself. This process may seem more like a messy sort of play to you, but it is important to give young children freedom to explore their food.

Exploring texture

At this age, your baby may well be on the way to eating three main meals a day so that she receives a combination of starchy food, vegetable or animal protein, and fruit or vegetables. She will manage coarser textures (see pages 54-5), especially with the arrival of teeth to improve her chewing abilities (see page 52). She can master finger foods (see opposite), so keep up her energy level between meals with healthy snacks of sandwiches or fruit slices. Her diet can now include virtually all the foods the rest of the family eats, except lightly cooked eggs, nuts, shellfish, unpasteurized or soft cheese, and low-fat or high-fiber products. Indeed, many dishes can be shared by all the family as long as your baby's portion is unseasoned.

KEEPING UP HER MILK

Your baby may be drinking less milk as her appetite for solid food increases, but she still needs ⅔ pint (400ml) of her usual breast milk or formula per day (see page 34). If your baby has used bottles, try to decrease their use gradually so you can dispense with them altogether during the coming weeks. It helps if you give most milk-feedings in a cup, perhaps reserving a soothing bottle-feeding for bedtime.

HYGIENE

Once your baby is 10 months old and actively exploring her environment (which often involves her "tasting" every object she lays her hands upon), there seems little point in sterilizing feeding spoons. However, bottles, nipples, and cup spouts should be thoroughly washed and sterilized until she is a year old. Your baby's hands should also be washed before and after eating. This is particularly important now that she is probably using her hands to dip into her meals as well as for picking up finger foods.

MANUAL SKILLS
Your baby can now manage food with a lumpier texture and she'll pick out some of the pieces herself to pop in her mouth.

New independence

Your baby is now acquiring new physical skills: rolling, crawling, sitting, or even walking. Improved muscle power and hand-to-eye coordination skills allow her much more independent movement. Your baby will be delighted by the freedom her body is giving her and she will want to take the lead at mealtimes by feeding herself; she may even become impatient when you try to spoon-feed her and prefer to be helped with just the odd spoonful of food. She will probably be following a more predictable sleeping pattern, which helps regulate mealtimes.

ENCOURAGING SELF-FEEDING
Your baby will need progressively less help to eat, and may well prefer to spoon up soft foods for herself. If more puree seems to go on the floor or her lap than in her mouth, you could use a two-spoon system: give her a spoon to hold so that she can make her own attempts at eating, and use another spoon yourself to get some of the food into her mouth.

FINGER FOODS
Finger foods are excellent for teaching feeding and should begin to play a useful part in her diet; she will enjoy the freedom of movement they give her and will appreciate the fact that she can eat this kind of food without adult intervention. Let her try steamed or raw vegetable sticks with a cold dip, or a favorite puree with bread sticks as finger foods. Remember that finger foods should be firm enough for your baby to pick up, yet tender enough for her to chew and swallow easily. Just because your baby has teeth, it doesn't mean that she instinctively knows how to use them for chewing: young babies are quite likely to bite off a piece of food, try to swallow it whole, and choke, so they must not be left unsupervised when eating, even for a moment.

EXPERIMENTATION
The more you allow your baby to experiment, the quicker she will learn to feed herself. It may be a messy procedure, but you should not discourage her attempts or worry that her table manners are less than perfect. She will be quick to pick up any anxieties on your part and could soon turn mealtimes into a battleground. Allow her to explore the feel of the food and take her time over eating it.

He has fine-tuned his grip and is well on the way to independent feeding

PRACTICE
A suction-based bowl keeps the food in one place while he makes a studied attempt to load his spoon and bring it to his mouth without dropping it.

PERFECTION
Once he has learned to maneuver the spoon correctly, his confidence will grow and he will probably proudly resist all offers of assistance.

Teething

During the 3 months leading up to your baby's first birthday, she may cut several teeth, so it is still important to offer textured foods that will encourage her to chew. If vegetable finger foods are cooled in the refrigerator first, they will be especially soothing on her gums. Opinions differ as to how far teething affects a baby's well-being, but it is probable that teething could cause her some distress and even make her fussier than usual about her food. For a few days before each tooth breaks through the gum, you may notice a hard, whitish bump under the surface of the gum. She might dribble, so it is a good idea to put a little petroleum jelly around her mouth and chin to help prevent it from becoming dry and red. If her gums are particularly tender, she may reject being fed from a spoon, so offer her finger foods to eat instead.

DENTAL HYGIENE

Start brushing your baby's teeth as soon as they appear – at least twice a day, in the morning and at bedtime. Make brushing teeth fun, perhaps by giving your baby her own toothbrush to hold while you brush your teeth. Bend down and show her what you are doing and encourage her to copy you. Of course, she won't do a proper brushing, but it will give her the right idea.

GEL-FILLED TEETHING RING   VEGETABLE STICKS

COOLING SORE GUMS
Vegetable sticks, such as cucumber and carrot, can be chilled in the refrigerator and given to your baby to bite on. Alternatively, cool a teething ring in the refrigerator for him to bite on.

PREVENTING DECAY
For most children a mild-tasting fluoride toothpaste (varieties for children have a slightly lower fluoride content) and a good diet are sufficient to protect teeth. Avoid gimmicky flavored toothpaste, since it is more helpful in the long run for children to know the difference between the taste of bubble gum and the taste of conventional toothpaste. To limit the possibility of tooth decay, never fill bottles with anything but milk or water: that way you prevent prolonged contact of sugary or acidic fluids with the teeth and gums. However, milk itself does contain a form of sugar that could be corrosive if the teeth were never cleaned. Once your baby's teeth have been brushed at bedtime, don't give her sweet drinks or more food, because at night there is not enough saliva in the mouth to wash away harmful acid.

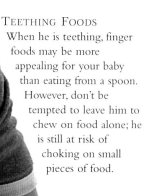

TEETHING FOODS
When he is teething, finger foods may be more appealing for your baby than eating from a spoon. However, don't be tempted to leave him to chew on food alone; he is still at risk of choking on small pieces of food.

Iron and growth

Babies are born with sufficient iron for the first six months of life, but after that they need to derive an adequate amount from their daily diet. Iron deficiency is in fact one of the most common nutritional problems in the world.

IRON DEFICIENCY

Iron deficiency can be difficult to spot since the symptoms are not so readily identifiable as those of an infectious illness. If symptoms of pallor, listlessness, and fatigue are missed, it can lead to anemia, which in turn results in poor energy levels. It should not be difficult to prevent this problem from occurring, or to eliminate it, by providing adequate dietary sources of iron.

DIETARY SOURCES OF IRON

Iron in foods of animal origin, such as red meat, particularly liver, or oily fish (salmon, sardines, or mackerel, for example), is much more easily absorbed than iron in foods of plant origin (see below for examples of iron-rich foods). However, if you include a good source of vitamin C at the same meal as a plant-based source of iron, you can improve the absorption of the iron. For example, a cup of fresh orange juice, slices of kiwi, a few chunks of sweet red pepper, or cauliflower are all vitamin C-rich foods and could be served at the same meal as a spinach or lentil dish. This would enable the iron in the latter to be better absorbed. Protein-rich foods also aid iron absorption. By mixing fish, lean red meat, or chicken with dark green leafy vegetables or lentils, you will improve the absorption of the vegetable sources of iron by about three times.

REMEMBER

◆ DO NOT OFFER your baby nuts, lightly cooked eggs, soft or unpasteurized cheeses, or shellfish.

◆ HONEY SHOULD NOT be given to babies under the age of 1 since in rare cases it can contain bacteria that cause botulism. However, if it is an ingredient in processed food, it is perfectly safe.

◆ ENCOURAGE YOUR BABY to drink from a cup, and offer only water, diluted juice, or her usual milk.

◆ OFFER FINGER FOODS as part of your baby's meals to give her chewing practice and encourage her to eat independently.

◆ AS SOON AS teeth appear, buy a mild toothpaste designed for children and brush your baby's teeth morning and night.

◆ DON'T OFFER tea, coffee, or cola drinks to your baby.

TOP IRON-RICH FOODS

LIVER AND RED MEATS

EGG YOLK (WELL-COOKED)

OILY FISH, FRESH OR CANNED (CHECK FOR BONES)

LEGUMES, SUCH AS LENTILS AND BAKED BEANS

BREAKFAST CEREALS FORTIFIED WITH IRON

BREAD AND RUSKS

GREEN LEAFY VEGETABLES, SUCH AS SPINACH AND CABBAGE

DRIED FRUITS, ESPECIALLY APRICOTS

A Varied Menu

TOWARD THE END of your baby's first year, solid food will replace much of her milk diet. It is important to introduce lots of different textures and flavors while your baby is so receptive to new foods. Offer some food mashed, some whole, some grated, and some diced: it's surprising what a few teeth and strong gums can manage. Finger foods that allow your baby to feed herself will become an increasingly important part of her daily diet, and will get her used to many new textures.

QUICK CHICKEN COUSCOUS
Couscous, made from crushed semolina, has a mild taste and soft texture that is perfect for babies. It is also very quick to cook and combines well with a variety of vegetables and even fruit. (See page 60 for recipe.)

CHEESY PASTA STARS
Tiny stars or other soup pasta shapes make an ideal introduction to pasta. Here they are combined with a tomato sauce enriched with grated Cheddar and sweetened with carrot. (See page 58 for recipe.)

FINGER FOODS

All finger foods should be firm enough for your baby to pick up, yet tender enough for her to chew and swallow easily. These foods are perfect for encouraging your child to eat independently, but never leave her alone while she is eating.

Cut cheese into novelty shapes

Chewing on chilled cucumber pieces may soothe sore gums

Toast shapes give good chewing practice

CREAMY AVOCADO DIP

This dip combines buttery, creamy-textured avocado with soft cream cheese. Serve with steamed vegetable shapes, such as sweet potato, or crunchy vegetable sticks and cheese or bread shapes.

(See page 56 for recipe.)

Offer soft pita bread strips and crunchy bread sticks

RED PEPPER DIP

This colorful puree of roasted red pepper, tomato, and cream cheese is served with raw vegetable sticks, which may be chilled to soothe gums made sore by teething. (See page 56 for recipe.)

Sweet, ripe, raw slices of apple and strawberry are excellent finger foods

RASPBERRY, PEAR & PEACH PUREE

A puree of mixed sweet, ripe fruits with mild, thick, plain yogurt makes a delicious summery dip. Offer raw fruit slices for dunking. (See page 57 for recipe.)

CREAMY AVOCADO DIP & VEGETABLE FINGERS

1 ripe avocado, halved and pitted

¼ cup (60g) soft cream cheese

1 tbsp snipped fresh chives

1 tomato, peeled, seeded, and chopped

STEAMED VEGETABLE SHAPES

vegetables such as sweet potato, carrot, potato, and parsnip, washed and peeled

An avocado has the highest protein content of any fruit, and babies like its mild creaminess. This dip also makes a good sandwich filling if mixed with grated cheese or chopped watercress.

1 Cut the vegetables into sticks or shapes, place in a steamer, and cook until tender, about 8 minutes.

2 Scoop out the avocado flesh. Mash until smooth and mix with the remaining ingredients. (For adults you can add lemon juice, seasoning, chopped cilantro, and maybe a little finely chopped chili.)

 Preparation/cooking
10 minutes/8 minutes

 Makes 4 portions

 Nutritional information
Rich source of folic acid, vitamin A, vitamin C, and vitamin E.

See page 55 for illustration.

RED PEPPER DIP & VEGETABLE FINGERS

1 small red pepper, halved and seeded

½ tbsp vegetable oil

1 shallot, peeled and finely chopped

1 tomato, peeled, seeded, and chopped

7oz (200g) cream cheese

RAW VEGETABLE SHAPES

vegetables such as carrot, celery, cucumber, pepper, and kohlrabi, washed and peeled

The vegetables for this dip should be cut into pieces small enough to be easily grasped, but not so tiny that they could be swallowed whole. You can also offer toast, pita fingers, or mild cheese shapes.

1 To make the dip, roast the red pepper, then peel and roughly chop.

2 Meanwhile, heat the oil in a small skillet, add the shallot, and sauté until softened but not colored. Combine the red pepper with the shallot, tomato, and cream cheese and blend together to make a smooth cream.

3 Cut the raw vegetables into strips, or make novelty shapes using miniature cookie cutters.

 Preparation/cooking
10 minutes/10 minutes

 Makes 4 portions

 Nutritional information
Rich source of beta-carotene, vitamin B12, and vitamin C.

See page 55 for illustration.

TIP
If your baby finds raw vegetables hard, offer steamed cauliflower or root vegetables. Reduce the steaming time progressively.

EASY MASHED VEGETABLE DUO

½lb (250g) rutabaga, chopped

1 cup (125g) chopped parsnips

1 cup (250ml) milk

¼ cup (30g) grated Cheddar cheese

This recipe makes both a good smooth puree and a slightly coarser textured dish.

Place the vegetables in a saucepan with the milk. Bring to a boil, cover, and simmer for 20 minutes, or until soft. Remove from the heat and stir in the cheese until melted. Mash to the desired consistency.

 Preparation/cooking
10 minutes/22 minutes

 Makes 4 portions

 Nutritional information
Rich source of calcium, folic acid, vitamin A, vitamin B12, and vitamin C.

 Suitable for freezing

FRUITY BABY MUESLI

¼ cup (30g) rolled oats

2 tbsp (30g) toasted wheat germ

1 dried apricot or pear, chopped

1 tbsp golden raisins

⅔ cup (150ml) white grape juice or apple juice

½ red apple, peeled and grated

3 seedless grapes, halved

Oats raise blood sugar relatively slowly, so oat-based breakfast cereals provide a more sustained energy boost than other cereals.

1 Put the oats and wheat germ in a bowl with the dried apricot and raisins. Cover with the grape juice. Let soak for at least 2 hours or overnight.

2 Add the apple and grapes to the soaked cereal and blend. (Once your baby has mastered the art of chewing, there is no need to blend this muesli.)

 Preparation
10 minutes, plus 2–12 hours soaking

 Makes 2 portions

 Nutritional information
Rich source of fiber, iron, B vitamins, vitamin C, and zinc.

APPLE & DATE OATMEAL

1 eating apple, peeled, cored, and chopped

¼ cup (45g) dates

4 tbsp water

⅔ cup (150ml) milk

2 tbsp (15g) rolled oats

1 Put the apple and dates in a pan with the water and cook over medium heat for 5 minutes.

2 Meanwhile, heat the milk in a pan, stir in the oats, bring to a boil, and simmer, stirring constantly, for 3–4 minutes, or until thickened. Mix with the fruit, then blend to the desired consistency.

 Preparation/cooking
2 minutes/12 minutes

 Makes 2 portions

 Nutritional information
Rich source of calcium, folic acid, and vitamin B12.

EXOTIC FRUIT SALAD

½ mango, peeled and pitted

½ papaya, peeled and pitted

1 kiwi, peeled

2 litchis, peeled and pitted

juice of 1 large orange

If you can't find perfectly ripe, sweet, exotic fruits, substitute peaches or strawberries.

Finely chop all the fruit and simply combine with the orange juice.

 Preparation
10 minutes

 Makes 4 portions

 Nutritional information
Rich source of beta-carotene and vitamin C.

RASPBERRY, PEAR & PEACH PUREE

½ cup (125g) raspberries

2 ripe pears, peeled, cored, and chopped

1 peach, peeled and chopped

2 tbsp plain yogurt

See page 55 for illustration.

This is very much a summer puree, to be made when raspberries and peaches are ripe and sweet. It is also good mixed with infant rice or mashed banana.

Place the fruits in a saucepan and simmer gently for about 5 minutes. Cool slightly, press through a strainer, and mix with the yogurt.

 Preparation/cooking
5 minutes/10 minutes

 Makes 4 portions

 Nutritional information
Rich source of fiber, folic acid, and vitamin C.

 Suitable for freezing

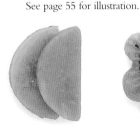

BUTTERNUT SQUASH WITH ALPHABET PASTA

10oz (300g) butternut squash, peeled and cubed

2–3 tbsp alphabet soup pasta

2 tbsp (30g) butter

½ tbsp chopped fresh sage

1 Put the squash in a steamer and cook until tender, about 15 minutes. Blend to a puree with 4–5 tablespoons of water from the bottom of the steamer.

2 Meanwhile, bring a pot of water to a boil, add the pasta, and cook until tender, about 5 minutes, then drain. Melt the butter in a pan, add the sage, and cook gently for 1 minute. Mix the sage butter with the squash and pasta.

 Preparation/cooking
5 minutes/20 minutes

 Makes 4 portions

 Nutritional information
Rich source of beta-carotene, folic acid, and vitamin C.

 Suitable for freezing

CHEESY PASTA STARS

1 cup (125g) carrots, sliced

1 cup (200ml) boiling water

2 tbsp (30g) butter

7oz (200g) tomatoes, peeled, seeded, and chopped

⅓ cup (45g) grated Cheddar cheese

2 tbsp soup pasta stars (stelline)

Tiny pasta stelline make a good introduction to pasta. The sweet taste of the carrots in this sauce is usually very appealing to babies.

1 Place the carrots in a small pan, cover with the boiling water, and cook until tender, 15–20 minutes. Melt the butter in a separate pan, add the tomatoes, and sauté until mushy. Remove from the heat and stir in the cheese until melted.

2 Meanwhile, bring a pot of water to a boil, add the pasta, and cook until tender, about 5 minutes, then drain.

3 Mix together the cooked carrots with their cooking liquid and the cheese and tomato sauce. Blend to a puree, then combine with the pasta stars.

 Preparation/cooking
10 minutes/25 minutes

 Makes 4 portions

 Nutritional information
Rich source of beta-carotene, calcium, folic acid, protein, vitamin B12, and vitamin C.

 Suitable for freezing

See page 54 for illustration.

TOMATO & MASCARPONE PASTA SAUCE

1 tbsp olive oil

1 shallot, finely chopped

1 garlic clove, crushed

1½ cups (400g) canned chopped tomatoes

1 tbsp tomato paste

1 tsp balsamic vinegar

½ tsp sugar

½ tsp mixed herbs

3 tbsp mascarpone cheese

Mascarpone is an Italian fresh cream cheese. This sauce goes well with pasta and is also good served with chicken. To adapt the sauce for adults, I would add a little chopped red chili at the same time as the shallot and garlic, and season to taste with salt and freshly ground black pepper.

1 Heat the oil in a saucepan, add the shallot and garlic, and sauté for 2 minutes.

2 Add the remaining ingredients except the mascarpone and cook over medium heat for about 15 minutes.

3 Puree the sauce in a blender and stir in the mascarpone cheese.

 Preparation/cooking
5 minutes/20 minutes

 Makes 4 portions

 Nutritional information
Rich source of folic acid.

 Suitable for freezing

FILLET OF FISH MORNAY WITH VEGETABLES

1 tbsp (15g) butter

½ cup (60g) finely sliced leeks

1 cup (125g) chopped carrots

¾ cup (60g) broccoli, cut into small florets

¼ cup (45g) fresh or frozen peas

5oz (150g) cod, flounder, or haddock fillets, skinned

⅔ cup (150ml) milk

3 peppercorns, 1 bay leaf, and a sprig of parsley

3 tsp (20g) butter

1 tbsp all-purpose flour

⅓ cup (45g) grated Cheddar or Edam cheese

This tasty combination of white fish and vegetables in a mild cheese sauce is generally very popular with babies.

1 Melt the butter in a saucepan, add the leeks, and sauté for 2–3 minutes. Add the carrots, cover with water, and cook for 10 minutes. Add the broccoli and cook for 5 minutes. Stir in the peas and simmer for 5 minutes longer or until the vegetables are tender (adding a little more water, if necessary).

2 Meanwhile, put the fish in a pan with the milk, peppercorns, bay leaf, and parsley. Simmer for 5 minutes, or until the fish is cooked. Set aside, reserving the cooking liquid. Discard the herbs.

3 To prepare the sauce, melt the butter in a pan, stir in the flour, and cook for 1 minute. Gradually whisk in the fish cooking liquid, bring to a boil, and cook until the sauce has thickened. Remove from the heat, add the cheese, and stir until melted.

4 Drain the vegetables and mix with the flaked fish and cheese sauce. Blend to a puree of the desired consistency for young babies. Provided the vegetables are tender, this can be mashed or chopped for older babies who are starting to chew.

 Preparation/cooking
10 minutes/35 minutes

 Makes 8 portions

 Nutritional information
Rich source of beta-carotene, calcium, folic acid, protein, vitamin B6, vitamin B12, and vitamin C.

 Suitable for freezing

FLAKED COD WITH TOMATOES & ZUCCHINI

5oz (150g) cod fillet, skinned

½ cup (100ml) milk

2 tbsp (30g) butter

1 shallot, chopped

1 small zucchini, chopped

¾lb (375g) tomatoes, peeled, seeded, and chopped

½ cup (60g) grated Cheddar cheese

1. Place the fish in a saucepan, cover with the milk, and poach gently for about 6 minutes.

2. Meanwhile, melt the butter in a pan, add the shallot, and cook until softened. Add the zucchini and sauté for 5 minutes. Add the tomatoes and sauté for 5 minutes more, or until mushy. Remove from the heat and stir in the cheese until melted.

3. Flake the fish carefully, checking for bones, and stir it into the tomato and zucchini sauce. For babies who don't yet like lumpy food, blend the mixture to a smoother consistency.

 Preparation/cooking
10 minutes/20 minutes

 Makes 4 portions

 Nutritional information
Rich source of beta-carotene, calcium, folic acid, protein, vitamin B6, vitamin B12, and vitamin C.

 Suitable for freezing

——— TIP ———
The cod can be microwaved on a high setting for 3 minutes.

CALIFORNIA CHICKEN

1½oz (45g) cooked chicken

1 tomato, peeled, seeded, and chopped

1oz (30g) avocado

2 tbsp mild plain yogurt

1½ tbsp grated Cheddar cheese

Use these ingredients to make yourself a salad or sandwich at the same time as a quick and easy meal for your baby. You can substitute Edam for Cheddar cheese.

Chop the chicken, then combine it with the remaining ingredients. Blend the mixture to the desired consistency.

 Preparation
10 minutes

 Makes 1 portion

 Nutritional information
Rich source of calcium, folic acid, protein, vitamin A, B vitamins, vitamin C, vitamin E, and zinc.

QUICK CHICKEN COUSCOUS

3 tsp (20g) butter

½ cup (60g) finely chopped leeks

2oz (60g) chicken, diced

¼ cup (30g) diced parsnips

¼ cup (30g) diced carrots

1 cup (250ml) unsalted chicken stock (see page 46)

½ cup (100g) couscous

If you prefer, replace the chicken with extra seasonal vegetables.

1. Melt the butter in a pan, add the leeks, and sauté for 5 minutes, or until softened. Add the chicken and sauté until just cooked through.

2. Meanwhile, place the parsnips and carrots in a steamer, or in a saucepan with boiling water to cover, and cook until tender, about 10 minutes.

3. Bring the stock to a boil in a pan. Stir in the couscous, remove from the heat, cover, and leave for 5 minutes, or until the stock has been absorbed. Fluff with a fork and stir in the chicken and vegetables. Add extra stock or water if necessary.

 Preparation/cooking
10 minutes/20 minutes

 Makes 4 portions

 Nutritional information
Rich source of beta-carotene, folic acid, iron, and protein.

See page 54 for illustration.

FRUITY CHICKEN WITH CARROTS

1 tbsp (15g) butter

2 tbsp (30g) finely chopped onion

2½oz (75g) boneless, skinless chicken, chopped

1 cup (125g) sliced carrots

½ eating apple, peeled, cored, and chopped

⅔ cup (150ml) unsalted chicken stock (see page 46)

Apple blends well with chicken to produce a lovely flavor in this quick-to-prepare dish. Well-cooked rice makes a good accompaniment.

1 Heat the butter in a pan, add the onion, and sauté for 3–4 minutes. Add the chicken and sauté until it turns opaque. Add the carrots and cook for 2 minutes, then stir in the chopped apple and pour in the chicken stock.

2 Bring the mixture to a boil, then cover and cook over medium heat for about 15 minutes. Chop or puree to the desired consistency.

 Preparation/cooking 10 minutes/22 minutes

 Makes 4 portions

 Nutritional information Rich source of beta-carotene, niacin, protein, and vitamin B6.

 Suitable for freezing

CREAMY CHICKEN & BROCCOLI

½ cup (90g) small broccoli florets

4oz (125g) cooked chicken, chopped

MILD CHEESE SAUCE

2 tbsp (30g) butter

2 tbsp all-purpose flour

1¼ cups (300ml) milk

½ cup (60g) grated Edam or other mild cheese

You could add some small cooked soup pasta, such as stelline, to this recipe to make it more substantial.

1 To prepare the cheese sauce, melt the butter in a saucepan, stir in the flour, and cook for 1 minute. Gradually whisk in the milk, bring to a boil, and cook until the sauce has thickened. Remove from the heat, add the cheese, and stir until melted.

2 Meanwhile, steam or microwave the broccoli until tender. Combine the cheese sauce, chicken, and broccoli. Then roughly chop the mixture in a blender or by hand.

 Preparation/cooking 5 minutes/15 minutes

 Makes 4 portions

 Nutritional information Rich source of calcium, folic acid, niacin, protein, vitamin A, vitamin B6, vitamin B12, and vitamin C.

 Suitable for freezing

— TIP —
If your baby doesn't like cheese, make a white sauce flavored with a pinch of nutmeg.

BABY'S BOLOGNESE

1 tbsp vegetable oil

2 tbsp (30g) finely chopped onion

1 tbsp (15g) finely chopped celery

2 tbsp (30g) grated carrots

¼lb (125g) lean ground beef

½ tsp tomato paste

2 tomatoes, peeled, seeded, and chopped

⅓ cup (90ml) unsalted chicken stock (see page 46)

1½oz (45g) spaghetti

1 Heat the oil in a pan, add the onion and celery, and sauté for 3–4 minutes. Add the grated carrots and cook for 2 minutes.

2 Add the ground beef and stir until browned. Stir in the tomato paste, tomatoes, and stock. Bring the mixture to a boil, reduce the heat, cover, and cook for 10–15 minutes, or until the meat is cooked through.

3 Meanwhile, bring a pot of water to a boil, add the spaghetti, and cook until soft, about 10 minutes. Drain and chop into small pieces. Transfer the bolognese sauce to a blender and puree to a fairly smooth, uniform texture before combining it with the pasta.

 Preparation/cooking 10 minutes/35 minutes

 Makes 6 portions

 Nutritional information Rich source of beta-carotene, folic acid, niacin, protein, vitamin B12, and zinc.

 Suitable for freezing sauce only

— TIP —
Babies sometimes find the chewy texture of red meat unpleasant, so I like to puree this sauce in a blender before serving it.

12-18 Months

Your child can now enjoy a full, varied diet and it should be easier to integrate him into family meals. Accordingly, the recipes in this chapter are designed to appeal to your toddler, but also suit the tastes of the whole family. You may find that your child needs quick, energy-boosting snacks, and so there are many suggestions for healthy snacks in this and the following chapters.

Changing Needs

YOUR BABY IS BECOMING MOBILE and will seem to have boundless energy. By now, he can enjoy the varied mixed diet that insures an adequate supply of the nutrients essential for his growth. However, young children's individual dietary needs vary considerably at this stage: some seem to consume vast quantities of food, others thrive on surprisingly little.

Balancing a mixed diet

At around 12 months old, your baby may look quite chubby, but once he gets up on his feet, he will slim down. When he is fully mobile, he will need snacks between meals to fuel his energy. As long as you encourage him to eat a variety of snacks, such as fruit, bites of cheese, or home-made cake, they will make up a useful part of his mixed diet.

CHILDREN'S NUTRITION

Although your child will be joining in with family meals, the dietary advice that applies to you as an adult will not necessarily be appropriate for him. Young children have different nutritional needs and require enough calories to sustain the growth of muscle, tissue, and bone that takes place during childhood. Advice concerning adult fat and fiber intake, for example, does not apply to the under 5s. While health experts tell us that adults and children over 5 should derive no more than 30 percent of their calories from fat, they also agree that we should not limit fat in the

diets of children under 2. Due to the very fast rate of growth in the first two years of life, fat is needed because it is the most concentrated source of energy. Without enough fat in the diet, a child would need to burn up protein for energy. Fat is also important for the healthy development of the brain and nervous system. Unless you have been advised by a doctor to do so, don't give your child reduced fat products such as 1 or 2 percent milk. In fact, your child still needs about ⅔ pint (400ml) of milk a day, although now he can stop breast milk or formula and drink whole milk (see opposite). A high-fiber diet, too, is still not appropriate for your child. Young children have small stomachs: fiber is low-calorie bulky material that fills the stomach without meeting a toddler's high calorific needs, and it can even hinder absorption of vital nutrients.

MILK INTAKE
Encourage your child to drink milk from a training cup rather than a bottle. However, she doesn't always need milk; water is a much better thirst-quencher.

KEEPING MILK IN THE DIET

If your child drinks milk reluctantly and you are worried that he is not getting the recommended ⅔ pint (400ml) of milk per day, you can easily smuggle milk into his meals. Yogurt, fromage frais, or pasteurized cheese can be used as substitutes. Alternatively, offer a fruity milkshake (see page 98), make a cheese sauce (see page 71) for part of the main meal, mash some potatoes with plenty of milk, or whip half-set gelatin with a can of evaporated milk.

DAIRY PRODUCTS IN THE DIET

FROMAGE FRAIS
OR YOGURT

CHEESE – SLICED, GRATED
ON PASTA OR ON TOAST

WHITE SAUCE IN FISH PIE
OR MACARONI AND CHEESE

MILK PUDDINGS, LIKE RICE
PUDDING OR TAPIOCA

HIGH-QUALITY
ICE CREAM

FRUITY OR CHOCOLATE
MILKSHAKES

A healthy eating plan for life

Health experts recommend we all try to include five portions of fruits or vegetables (not including potatoes) in our diet each day. It is believed that this helps protect against certain forms of cancer and heart disease, and provides the correct balance of nutrients. If you start your baby on this eating plan, you will set him on the road to a healthy diet for life.

IMPLEMENTING THE PLAN

It is not as difficult as it sounds to incorporate five helpings of fresh fruits or vegetables in the daily diet: some fresh or cooked fruit with breakfast, a serving of vegetables and a glass of fruit juice with lunch, and a serving of vegetables at dinnertime, followed by fresh fruit or a fruit pudding makes five helpings (see below).

VEGETABLE REJECTION

Often children raise strong objections to eating vegetables. They may dislike the distinctive taste – the strong flavor of broccoli, for example – or they may find a vegetable's texture off-putting. If you encounter this problem, you could offer fresh fruits, which also provide vitamins, and which can accompany a savory dish equally well. At other meals, gradually introduce some of the more popular vegetables into your child's diet, such as carrots, corn, and potatoes. Children often prefer raw vegetables to cooked, so you could offer carrot sticks, celery, or cucumber pieces. Alternatively, hide vegetables among other ingredients, as in my Pasta Sauce with Hidden Vegetables (see page 72).

FIVE-STAR EATING PLAN

MUESLI WITH FRESH
FRUIT FOR BREAKFAST

A MID-MORNING SNACK
OF FRESH FRUIT

PASTA WITH BROCCOLI
AND CHEESE FOR LUNCH

A DIP WITH VEGETABLE
STICKS FOR SNACK

CHICKEN SALAD
SANDWICHES FOR DINNER

Making meals fun

Young children, like adults, prefer to eat with company. If your toddler has cutlery he is able to use, is seated at the correct height, and has someone to share the meal with, mealtimes will be an enjoyable occasion for him. You may find that he will eat things he has previously rejected just because a sibling or friend is eating it. Visiting a friend or relative's house often produces the same effect. The excitement of eating in different surroundings or with other children makes him adventurous enough to try new foods. When you and your child are with other people you may both be more relaxed about the food you are eating. When you are on your own with him, there is a certain amount of unconscious pressure for your child if you are overseeing every mouthful he takes. Consequently, meals can become an ordeal. It is easy for both of you to forget that eating should be fun.

A booster seat brings your toddler to the correct table level

EATING SOCIABLY AT HOME
Eating as a family will help your child integrate into regular mealtimes as well as learn some of your basic family rules about eating at the table. Even if the whole family can't sit down together at meals during the week – perhaps because the meal is too late for your young child to join in more than occasionally – do sit down beside him while he eats, or ask an older sibling or friend to join him.

COOKING FOR THE FAMILY
By now your toddler should be eating the same meals as the rest of the family. Life is too short to cook a different meal for every member of the family and it is much easier to accustom children to new foods at this early age, when their preferences (and prejudices) are not yet fixed. You can interest him in food, perhaps by talking to him about its form, taste, or feel, or by adding a few presentational touches that will appeal to him. However, don't get overanxious or angry if he refuses to eat a new dish and don't threaten him with no dessert. Instead, make sure that the dessert is nutritious (see page 78) so that you can relax in the knowledge that he is still eating a healthy diet, even if it's not in the traditional order. Remember that the "balance" of a diet should be assessed over a period of a few days to a week, rather than within a strict limit of 24 hours.

ENCOURAGING SOCIAL SKILLS
Eating with young friends and family makes mealtimes fun and encourages children to eat things they may otherwise turn down.

REMEMBER
◆ YOU CAN NOW introduce whole milk as your child's usual milk, unless he has special dietary needs.

◆ OFFER PLAIN WATER as a thirst-quencher or give well-diluted fruit or vegetable juice (using approximately two thirds water to one third juice).

◆ IF YOUR BABY has not already learned to drink from a cup, try to get him off the bottle now.

◆ ENCOURAGE YOUR CHILD to eat plenty of fruits and vegetables as part of his meals and as between-meal snacks.

◆ OFFER SIMPLE, easy-to-digest foods after illnesses. Recognize that your child may revert to slightly babyish feeding habits for a short period of time.

When your child is unwell

When children are unwell, they often lose their appetite. However, it is important to ensure that your child's fluid intake is maintained. Approximately 80 percent of a new baby is made up of water (adults are around 70 percent). Consequently, babies and young children are particularly vulnerable to dehydration during periods of diarrhea or vomiting. If a child is suffering from either of these problems, stop giving solids and offer plenty of fluids. Special salt and sugar powders that are dissolved in water replace lost minerals and can be bought at drugstores. Diluted fruit juices, ice pops, or flat soda (take the bubbles out first with ice or a swizzle stick) are suitable for children with diarrhea. Milk is not suitable.

FOODS DURING ILLNESS

If your child is sick but not suffering from diarrhea or vomiting, give liquids that are nutritious – milk, milkshakes (see page 98), or hot chocolate are good. Ice pops made from fresh fruit juice, pureed fruit, or yogurt are also suitable. Offer simple, easily digested foods, such as homemade chicken soup, steamed fish and mashed potatoes, scrambled egg on toast, or mashed banana. Antibiotics kill the good bacteria in the body as well as the harmful ones. If your child is taking antibiotics, you could give him yogurt to help maintain the levels of beneficial bacteria in the body.

CONSTIPATION

If your child is constipated, give him plenty of water and diluted fruit juices. Cut down on sugary and fatty foods and offer fruit, vegetables, and whole grain cereals, but do not overload the digestive system with fiber since this is not a suitable way to relieve constipation in young children. Yogurt, prunes, and prune juice are more useful in gently relieving it.

REGRESSION

Don't be surprised if your child reverts to more babyish feeding habits even after he has recovered from being ill. While he is ill, he needs extra reassurance in the form of hugs and he may want his drinks from a bottle again. Until his appetite returns, the memory of his more babyish comforts may make him want to eat the kinds of things you thought he had outgrown. (In fact, this may be the case throughout his early childhood whenever your child is ill.) Try not to worry, he'll soon be back to his old self with a healthy appetite ready to try out new foods again.

DURING ILLNESS
Keep your child's fluid intake high during illness. While he is unwell, he may want to use a bottle or training cup that he had previously given up as a kind of comforter.

Food for the Senses

ENCOURAGING YOUR TODDLER to explore the tastes, textures, and even the different sounds particular foods make when munched, scrunched, and bitten will stimulate his interest in food and heighten his enjoyment of mealtimes. Even before language skills are very developed, your child will be capable of expressing his responses to new foods, and will enjoy being given plenty of freedom to explore his food with his hands. The foods on these pages are designed to appeal to the eye, to the sense of smell, touch, and hearing, and, of course, to the tastebuds.

CHICKEN SAUSAGE SNAILS

With the help of a little imagination, a simple dish of chicken sausages and mashed potatoes becomes an eye-catching picture on a plate and an appealing meal. (See page 75 for recipe.)

ROOT VEGETABLE CHIPS

A satisfying crunch is produced by these deep-fried chips of sweet potato, beet, and parsnip. (See page 70 for recipe.)

TURKEY BALLS & PEPPER SAUCE

Chopped fresh basil perfumes and flavors the delicious sweet pepper sauce that accompanies these juicy miniature meatballs. This dish can be served on a bed of rice, but goes equally well with spaghetti. (See page 76 for recipe.)

Show your toddler how to scrunch a sprig of fresh basil in his hands, then sniff the bruised leaves

YOGURT PANCAKES
The contrast of sticky maple syrup, ripe summer fruit, and warm pancakes is appealing. (See page 78 for recipe.)

RASPBERRY FROZEN YOGURT
Scoops of frosty, frozen yogurt decorated with chocolate chips and brittle wafers make a mouth-watering, and tactile, dessert. (See page 78 for recipe.)

APRICOT & BLUEBERRY OATMEAL

1½ cups (350ml) milk

¾ cup (90g) rolled oats

⅓ cup (90g) ready-to-eat dried apricots, chopped

¾ cup (90g) blueberries

This makes a simple, nutritious breakfast for your baby. There's no need to blend it for older children.

Pour the milk into a saucepan, bring to a boil, and stir in the oats and apricots. Reduce the heat and cook for 3 minutes, stirring. Stir in the blueberries and cook for 2 more minutes. Blend for a few seconds to the desired consistency.

 Preparation/cooking
2 minutes/7 minutes

 Makes 4 portions

 Nutritional information
Rich source of calcium, folic acid, iron, protein, and zinc.

ROOT VEGETABLE CHIPS

1 orange-fleshed sweet potato, scrubbed

1 parsnip, peeled

2 carrots or 1 raw beet, peeled

oil for deep frying

freshly ground sea salt

Encourage your child to eat more vegetables by making these crunchy chips. They make a healthy alternative to potato chips.

1 Slice all the vegetables wafer thin by hand or by using a slicing blade attachment in a food processor. Heat the oil in a deep-fat fryer or deep pan to 375°F/190°C. Add each vegetable separately, in small batches, and fry until crisp and golden, 4–5 minutes if using a deep-fat fryer.

2 Remove from the oil and drain on paper towels. Sprinkle with sea salt and serve cold.

 Preparation/cooking
10 minutes/15 minutes

 Makes 4 portions

 Nutritional information
Rich source of beta-carotene, fiber, folic acid, and vitamin E.

See page 68 for illustration.

──── TIP ────
You can also make these chips using sliced plantain.

ZUCCHINI & TOMATO FRITTATA

2 tbsp vegetable oil

1 onion, chopped

1¼ cup (175g) zucchini, thinly sliced

salt and pepper, to taste

2 tomatoes, peeled, seeded, and chopped

4 eggs

1 tbsp milk

2 tbsp freshly grated Parmesan

1 Heat the oil in a 9½in (24cm) nonstick skillet. Add the onion and zucchini, season lightly, and cook for about 15 minutes. Add the tomatoes and continue to cook for 3–4 minutes.

2 Beat the eggs with the milk and pepper and pour over the vegetables. Cook over medium heat for about 5 minutes, or until the eggs are set underneath. Preheat the broiler to high.

3 Sprinkle the Parmesan over the frittata and cook briefly in the broiler until golden (if necessary, wrap the pan handle with foil to prevent burning). Cut into wedges and serve hot or cold.

VARIATIONS

Omit the zucchini and tomatoes. Add ¼lb (125g) cooked diced ham and ½ cup (75g) peas to the beaten egg mixture.

Omit the zucchini. Add 1 small diced and sautéed red pepper and 2 cubed boiled potatoes to the egg.

 Preparation/cooking
5 minutes/30 minutes

 Makes 8 portions

 Nutritional information
Rich source of calcium, folic acid, protein, vitamin A, vitamin B12, and vitamin C.

PASTA CARTWHEELS WITH CHEESE & BROCCOLI

4oz (125g) pasta cartwheels

¼lb (125g) broccoli, cut into small florets

⅓ cup (60g) frozen corn

CHEESE SAUCE

2 tbsp (30g) butter

¼ cup (30g) flour

1¼ cups (300ml) milk

pinch of nutmeg

½ cup (75g) grated Cheddar cheese

salt and pepper, to taste

TOPPING

2 tbsp freshly grated Parmesan

1½ tbsp fresh bread crumbs

1 Bring a pot of lightly salted water to a boil, add the pasta, and cook until tender, about 8 minutes, or according to package instructions. Drain and set aside.

2 Meanwhile, place the broccoli and corn in a steamer and cook for 4–5 minutes, or until tender. Cover to keep warm and set aside.

3 To make the sauce, melt the butter in a small pan. Add the flour to make a paste and stir over low heat for 1 minute. Gradually whisk in the milk, bring slowly to a boil, and cook until thickened, stirring constantly. Remove from the heat. Add the nutmeg, stir in the Cheddar until melted, then season.

4 Stir the vegetables into the sauce, then mix with the pasta. Pour the mixture into a greased gratin dish and scatter the Parmesan and bread crumbs. Bake in the preheated oven for about 15 minutes.

VARIATION

To make macaroni and cheese, omit the vegetables and replace the cartwheels with 5oz (150g) macaroni.

 Preparation/cooking
10 minutes/35 minutes

 Oven temperature
350°F/180°C

 Makes 4 portions

 Nutritional information
Rich source of calcium, folic acid, protein, vitamin A, B vitamins, and zinc.

 Suitable for freezing
sauce only

PASTA & SAUCE WITH HIDDEN VEGETABLES

2 tbsp olive oil

1 small onion, chopped

1 garlic clove, crushed

½ cup (75g) chopped carrots

½ cup (75g) chopped zucchini

½ cup (75g) sliced mushrooms

1½ cups (400g) canned chopped tomatoes

½ cup (125ml) vegetable stock

¼ tsp brown sugar

salt and pepper, to taste

8oz (250g) pasta twists (fusilli)

If your baby is reluctant to eat vegetables, one solution is to resort to disguise. This sauce has lots of vegetables blended into it. Mix it with fun pasta shapes and you have a winner! A tablespoon of pesto makes a nice addition.

1 Heat the oil in a pan, add the onion and garlic, and sauté for about 3 minutes. Add the carrots, zucchini, and mushrooms and cook for about 15 minutes, or until softened. Add the tomatoes, stock, sugar, and seasoning to taste, and simmer for 10 minutes. Blend to a puree.

2 Meanwhile, bring a pot of lightly salted water to a boil, add the pasta, and cook until tender, about 10 minutes. Toss with the sauce and serve.

 Preparation/cooking 10 minutes/30 minutes

 Makes 4 portions

 Nutritional information Rich source of beta-carotene, folic acid, iron, protein, B vitamins, vitamin C, and vitamin E.

 Suitable for freezing sauce only

TUNA & ZUCCHINI LASAGNA

1 tbsp vegetable oil

1 onion, finely chopped

1 garlic clove, crushed (optional)

2 zucchini, trimmed and sliced

¾ cup (125g) frozen corn

1½ cups (400g) canned chopped tomatoes

1 cup (250ml) water

2 tbsp tomato paste

10oz (300g) canned tuna

1½ batches cheese sauce (see page 71)

9 sheets oven-ready lasagna

¼ cup (30g) grated Cheddar cheese, to finish

1 Heat the oil in a skillet, add the onion and garlic, if using, and sauté until softened. Stir in the zucchini and corn, and cook for 2 minutes.

2 Add the tomatoes, water, and tomato paste. Bring to a boil, then simmer for about 30 minutes. Remove from the heat, add the tuna to the sauce, and stir thoroughly. Make the cheese sauce and keep warm.

3 To assemble the lasagna, spoon one third of the tomato and tuna sauce onto the bottom of a 9 x 6 x 3½in (23 x 15 x 8cm) ovenproof dish. Lay 3 sheets of the lasagna on top, then spoon a third of the warm cheese sauce over the top.

4 Repeat the layering twice, ending with cheese sauce, and sprinkle the grated Cheddar cheese. Transfer the dish to the preheated oven and cook for about 30 minutes, or until the top is golden and bubbling.

 Preparation/cooking 10 minutes/1 hour 20 minutes

 Oven temperature 375°F/190°C

 Makes 8 portions

 Nutritional information Rich source of calcium, folic acid, protein, vitamin A, B vitamins, vitamin E, and zinc.

 Suitable for freezing

ORZO WITH COLORFUL DICED VEGETABLES

½ cup (90g) orzo

½ cup (60g) diced carrots

½ cup (60g) diced zucchini

½ cup (60g) diced broccoli

2 tbsp (30g) butter

¼ cup (30g) freshly grated
Cheddar or Parmesan cheese

Orzo is the name given to tiny pasta shapes that resemble barley kernels (you can also find riso or puntalette – "grains of rice"). Its creamy, slightly chewy texture is very appealing to children.

1 Put the pasta in a saucepan together with the diced vegetables, pour in enough boiling water to cover generously, and cook for about 12 minutes, or until all the vegetables are tender. Drain the pasta and vegetables thoroughly.

2 Melt the butter in a large pan, stir in the drained pasta and vegetables, then remove from the heat. Add the grated cheese and toss until the cheese has melted.

Preparation/cooking
10 minutes/15 minutes

Makes 4 portions

Nutritional information
Rich source of beta-carotene, folic acid, protein, and vitamin C.

Suitable for freezing

BOW-TIE PASTA WITH HAM & PEAS

5oz (150g) pasta bows
(farfalle)

½ vegetable bouillon cube

3 tsp (20g) butter

2 tbsp (15g) flour

1¼ cups (300ml) milk

¼ tsp dry mustard

½ cup (60g) frozen peas
(or a mixture of peas
and corn)

½ cup (60g) grated aged
Cheddar cheese

2oz (60g) sliced cooked ham,
cut into strips

salt and pepper, to taste

Bow-tie pasta is a good shape for young children – don't worry if they treat it as finger food. Good manners will come in time! This is also successful made with green and white narrow pasta noodles (tagliolini or taglierini).

1 Bring a pot of water to a boil, add the pasta and bouillon cube, and cook until tender, about 10 minutes, or according to package instructions.

2 Meanwhile, make the sauce. Melt the butter in a small pan, stir in the flour to make a paste, then gradually whisk in the milk and mustard. Stir in the peas and cook for 3 minutes. Remove from the heat and stir in the cheese until melted. Add the ham, heat through, season to taste, then toss with the pasta.

VARIATION

To make a vegetarian version, omit the ham and add 2½oz (75g) sliced mushrooms sautéed in a little butter until tender.

Preparation/cooking
5 minutes/15 minutes

Makes 4 portions

Nutritional information
Rich source of calcium, folic acid, protein, vitamin A, B vitamins, and zinc.

Suitable for freezing
sauce only

JOY'S FISH PIE

½lb (250g) each cod and salmon fillets, skinned

3¾ cups (900ml) milk

4 peppercorns, 1 bay leaf, and a parsley sprig

4 tbsp (60g) butter

1 onion, finely chopped

3 tbsp flour

1 tsp dry mustard

1 cup (125g) frozen peas

1 cup (125g) corn kernels

4 tbsp (60g) grated Cheddar

1 tbsp snipped fresh chives

salt and pepper, to taste

MASHED POTATOES

1½lb (750g) potatoes, cut into chunks

4 tbsp milk

1 tbsp (15g) butter

salt and pepper, to taste

A good fish pie with creamy mashed potatoes is one of those popular, old-fashioned comfort foods. This recipe comes from my friend Joy.

1 For the mashed potatoes, boil some lightly salted water, add the potatoes, and boil until tender.

2 Meanwhile, put the fish in a shallow pan with the milk, peppercorns, and herbs. Bring to a boil, then cover and cook for 5 minutes, or until the fish flakes easily. Remove the fish, strain the milk, and reserve. Flake the fish with a fork and set aside.

3 Melt the butter in a small pan, add the onion, and sauté until softened. Stir in the flour to make a paste and cook for 1 minute. Gradually add the strained milk, stirring until the sauce thickens.

4 Mix in the mustard, peas, corn, chives, and most of the Cheddar (keep 2 tbsp to sprinkle over the finished dish). Cook for 4 minutes. Season and add the fish. Put the mixture in an 11 x 7in (28 x 18cm) ovenproof dish.

5 Drain and mash the potatoes. Add milk, butter, and seasoning. Spread the potatoes over the fish, making peaks with a fork. Sprinkle with remaining cheese. Cook in the preheated oven for 25 minutes.

 Preparation/cooking
15 minutes/50 minutes

 Oven temperature
350°F/180°C

 Makes 8 portions

 Nutritional information
Rich source of calcium, folic acid, protein, vitamin A, B vitamins, and zinc.

 Suitable for freezing

TIP
For an interesting variation, add cooked shrimp to the fish. You can also make miniature portions in ramekin dishes.

CREAMY SEAFOOD WITH RICE

1 cup (175g) basmati rice, rinsed

¼lb (125g) each cod and salmon fillets, skinned

1¼ cups (300ml) milk

3 peppercorns, 1 bay leaf, and a parsley sprig

2 tbsp (30g) butter

1 small onion, finely chopped

2 heaping tbsp flour

¼ cup (30g) frozen peas

3oz (90g) cooked shrimp

¼ cup (30g) grated Cheddar

salt and pepper, to taste

1 tomato, peeled, seeded, and chopped

1 Bring a pot of lightly salted water to a boil. Add the rice and cook until tender, about 11 minutes.

2 Meanwhile, put the cod and salmon fillets in a shallow pan with the milk, peppercorns, and herbs. Bring to a boil, then cover and simmer for 5 minutes, or until the fish is cooked and flakes easily. Remove the fish with a slotted spoon, strain the milk, and reserve. Cut the fish into chunks.

3 Melt the butter in a small pan, add the onion, and sauté until just softened. Stir in the flour to make a paste and cook for 1 minute. Gradually add the strained milk, stirring until the sauce thickens.

4 Add the fish to the sauce with the frozen peas and shrimp, and heat through. Remove from the heat, stir in the grated cheese, and season to taste. Arrange a portion of fish on a bed of rice and sprinkle with some chopped tomato.

 Preparation/cooking
10 minutes/20 minutes

 Makes 4 portions

 Nutritional information
Rich source of folic acid, protein, B vitamins, incl. B12, and zinc.

 Suitable for freezing

TIP
This creamy sauce would also make a good sauce for pasta shells (conchiglie).

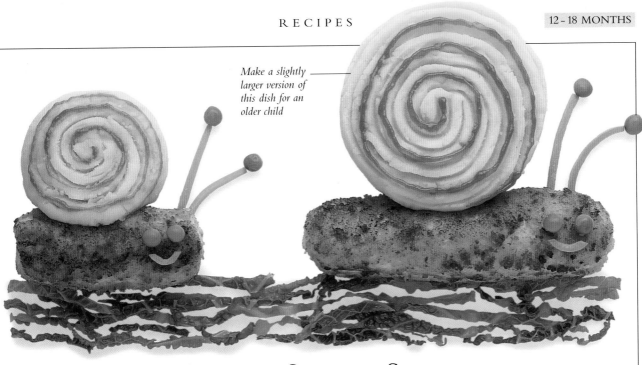

Make a slightly larger version of this dish for an older child

CHICKEN SAUSAGE SNAILS

CHICKEN SAUSAGES

¾lb (375g) raw, skinned, boneless chicken breast, cubed

1 small onion, finely chopped

½ tbsp chopped fresh parsley

½ chicken bouillon cube, finely crumbled

1 small apple, peeled and grated

2 tbsp fresh bread crumbs

salt and pepper, to taste

flour for coating

vegetable oil for frying

MASHED POTATOES

1lb (500g) potatoes, cut into chunks

1 tbsp milk

1 tbsp (15g) butter

salt and pepper, to taste

TO DECORATE

shredded savoy cabbage

1 carrot, cut into sticks

16 frozen peas

ketchup

Using a little imagination, you can make succulent homemade chicken sausages into a fun and visually appealing meal.

1 Put the chicken in a food processor with the onion, parsley, crumbled bouillon cube, apple, and bread crumbs. Chop for a few seconds, then season the mixture lightly.

2 Form the mixture into 4 sausages, each about 5in (12cm) long. Spread the flour on a plate and use to coat the sausages. Heat the vegetable oil in a skillet, add the sausages, and sauté for about 15 minutes, turning occasionally, or until browned on all sides and cooked through.

3 Meanwhile, place the potatoes in the bottom of a steamer, cover with lightly salted water, and cook until tender. Five minutes before the potatoes are done, put the vegetables for decorating in the top of the steamer and cook until tender. Mash the potatoes with the milk, butter, and seasoning.

4 To assemble, use an ice cream scoop to form the potatoes into 4 dome shapes. Decorate with a ketchup spiral to create a snail-shell effect (you can use a piping bag with a small nozzle for this, or cut a small hole in the corner of a freezer bag and use that). Put a sausage underneath each dome of potato. Use the steamed carrot sticks and peas to make the snail's feelers, and arrange the cabbage as grass.

 Preparation/cooking
20 minutes/1 hour
10 minutes

 Makes 4 portions

 Nutritional information
Rich source of folic acid, protein, B vitamins, and zinc.

 Suitable for freezing
chicken sausages only

TURKEY BALLS & PEPPER SAUCE

RED PEPPER SAUCE

1½ tbsp vegetable oil

2 shallots, finely chopped

1½ red peppers, seeded and chopped

1 tsp tomato paste

3 tbsp chopped fresh basil

2 cups (450ml) vegetable stock

salt and pepper, to taste

TURKEY MEATBALLS

1lb (500g) ground turkey

1 onion, finely chopped

1 small apple, peeled and grated

3 tbsp fresh bread crumbs

1 egg, lightly beaten

2 tbsp chopped fresh sage or thyme

salt and pepper, to taste

flour for coating

2 tbsp vegetable oil for frying

Served with rice or spaghetti, these little meatballs make a great lunch. If you have time, roast and skin the peppers for the sauce, which can also be made with chicken stock (see page 46).

1 To make the red pepper sauce, heat the oil in a skillet, add the shallots and red peppers, and sauté until softened. Stir in the remaining ingredients and season to taste. Bring to a boil and simmer for 15–20 minutes. Blend until smooth.

2 Mix together all the ingredients for the meatballs, seasoning to taste. Use your hands to form the mixture into about 24 walnut-size balls. Spread the flour on a plate and use to coat the meatballs. Heat the oil in a skillet, add the meatballs, and sauté until golden all over.

3 Transfer the meatballs to a casserole, cover with the pepper sauce, and cook in the preheated oven for about 20 minutes, or until the meatballs are cooked through and well browned.

 Preparation/cooking
20 minutes/40 minutes

 Oven temperature
350°F/180°C

 Makes 8 portions

 Nutritional information
Rich source of beta-carotene, folic acid, iron, protein, B vitamins, and zinc.

 Suitable for freezing

——— TIP ———
These can be made ahead and frozen, then simply defrosted and reheated in a microwave (just make sure you test the temperature before giving them to your child).

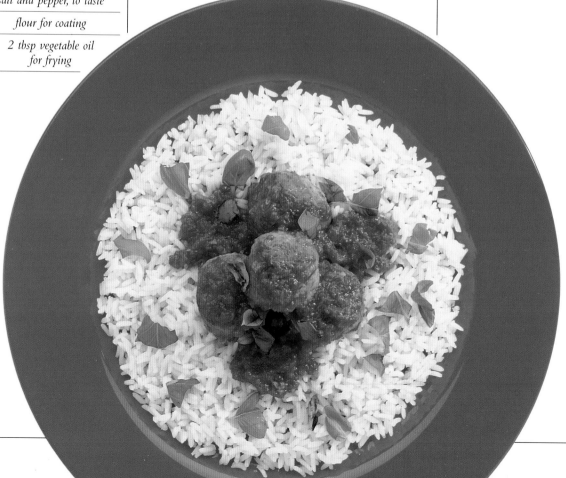

FINGER PICKING CHICKEN & POTATO BALLS

¼lb (125g) potatoes, chopped

1 cup (125g) chopped parsnips

3 tbsp vegetable oil

½ small onion, finely chopped

1 carrot, grated

¼lb (125g) boneless chicken breast, cut into chunks

1 tbsp (15g) butter

flour for coating

Mashed potatoes and parsnips give these balls a soft texture and a hint of sweetness, and they are just the right size for picking up and nibbling.

1 Put the potatoes and parsnips in a pan, cover with water, bring to a boil, then simmer, covered, for 12–15 minutes, or until tender.

2 Meanwhile, heat 1 tablespoon of oil in a skillet, add the onion and carrot, and sauté for 4–5 minutes. Add the chicken and continue to sauté for about 10 minutes, or until cooked through.

3 Drain the potatoes and parsnips and mash with half the butter until smooth. Finely chop the chicken, onion, and carrot in a food processor and mix with the mashed vegetables.

4 Form the mixture into about 24 walnut-size balls. Spread the flour on a plate and coat the balls. Heat the remaining oil and butter in a skillet, add the meatballs, and sauté until golden.

 Preparation/cooking
10 minutes/40 minutes

 Makes 8 portions

 Nutritional information
Rich source of beta-carotene, folic acid, and protein.

 Suitable for freezing

SHEPHERD'S PIE

1½ tbsp vegetable oil

1 large onion, chopped

1 small red pepper, finely chopped

1 garlic clove, crushed

1lb (500g) lean ground lamb

1¼ cups (300ml) chicken stock (see page 46) or beef stock

1 tbsp chopped fresh parsley

1 tbsp tomato paste

¼ tsp Worcestershire sauce

1¼ cups (175g) mushrooms, sliced

MASHED POTATOES

2lb (1kg) potatoes, chopped

3 tbsp (45g) butter

3 tbsp milk

salt and pepper, to taste

1 Heat the oil in a pan, add the onion, red pepper, and garlic, and sauté until softened. Add the meat and sauté until browned. If desired, transfer the cooked mixture to a food processor and chop for a few seconds on the pulse setting.

2 Transfer the meat to a saucepan and add the stock, parsley, tomato paste, Worcestershire sauce, and mushrooms. Cook over medium heat for about 20 minutes.

3 Meanwhile, boil the potatoes in lightly salted water until tender, then drain and mash with two-thirds of the butter and the milk. Season to taste.

4 Arrange the meat either in one large dish or in individual ramekins, cover with the mashed potatoes, and dot the topping with the remaining butter. Cook in the preheated oven for 20 minutes.

VARIATION

To make cottage pie, replace the ground lamb with the same quantity of lean ground beef. For the topping, omit the mashed potatoes and replace with 2lb (1kg) mashed rutabaga, or use a combination of mashed rutabaga and potato.

 Preparation/cooking
15 minutes/1 hour 10 minutes

 Oven temperature
350°F/180°C

 Makes 8 portions

 Nutritional information
Rich source of folic acid, iron, protein, vitamin A, B vitamins, and zinc.

 Suitable for freezing

—— TIPS ——

To make ground meat more palatable to young children, cook it first and then chop it in a food processor.

If preferred, make the shepherd's pie in individual ramekins and decorate with vegetable faces (see page 103).

RASPBERRY FROZEN YOGURT

½lb (250g) frozen or fresh raspberries

4 tbsp superfine sugar

½ cup (125ml) water

1¼–1½ cups (300–350ml) plain yogurt

6 tbsp crème fraîche

2–3 tbsp confectioners' sugar

This can also be made with a mixture of berries – perhaps strawberries, blackberries, and raspberries. A few minutes before you want to eat it, take it from the freezer and allow to soften slightly. Serve by itself or with some fresh raspberries.

1 Put the raspberries in a saucepan with the sugar and water. Bring to a simmer, then cook for 5 minutes. Puree using a hand blender, then strain through a sieve to get rid of the seeds. Let cool.

2 Stir the yogurt and crème fraîche into the raspberry puree and add enough confectioners' sugar to sweeten. Transfer to an ice cream maker and freeze for about 20 minutes.

VARIATION

Mix 1¾ cups (375ml) cherry yogurt with 6 tablespoons of crème fraîche. Stir in 7oz (200g) canned pitted black cherries, 6½ tbsp (100ml) maple syrup, and 1½oz (45g) grated semisweet chocolate. Transfer to an ice cream maker, and freeze as described above.

Preparation/cooking
2 minutes/35 minutes, incl. 20 minutes freezing

Makes 8 portions

Nutritional information
Rich source of calcium, folic acid, protein, vitamin B2, vitamin C, and vitamin B12.

See page 69 for main illustration.

---TIP---
If you don't have an ice cream maker, put the mixture in a plastic container. Freeze for 1 hour, then remove and beat by hand or in a food processor to break up the ice crystals. Freeze again, repeating the beating procedure once or twice during freezing.

YOGURT PANCAKES

1 egg, lightly beaten

⅔ cup (150ml) plain yogurt (not light)

⅔ cup (150ml) milk

¾ cup (100g) self-rising flour

¼ tsp salt, or 2 tbsp maple syrup (for a sweeter version)

vegetable oil for frying

TO ACCOMPANY

pure maple syrup

fresh fruit such as strawberries, raspberries, or sliced peaches

These mini pancakes are delicious served with fresh fruit and maple syrup. You could also add a few golden raisins to a maple syrup-sweetened batter to make raisin pancakes.

1 Mix together the beaten egg and the yogurt, then stir in the milk, flour, and salt or maple syrup. Mix until you have a smooth batter.

2 Heat a little oil in a skillet until sizzling hot. Drop heaping tablespoons of batter into the pan, leaving plenty of space around each one, and flatten slightly with a spatula. They should spread to about 2½in (6cm) across. Cook for 1–2 minutes until lightly browned, then turn and cook for a further 1–2 minutes until browned on the other side and set in the center.

3 Drizzle the pancakes with maple syrup and serve scattered with fruit.

Preparation/cooking
2 minutes/10 minutes

Makes 8 portions

Nutritional information
Rich source of calcium, folic acid, protein, vitamin B2, and vitamin B12 (served with fruit).

Suitable for freezing
See tip below

See page 69 for illustration.

---TIP---
These pancakes can be layered between pieces of waxed paper and then frozen. They can be reheated in a toaster.

BANANA CHIPS WITH HONEY YOGURT DIP

4 bananas, cut lengthwise into thin strips

confectioners' sugar mixed with a sprinkling of cinnamon (optional)

plain yogurt sweetened with honey

These fruit chips can also be made with mango. You could serve them with a fruity fromage frais dip.

1 Place the strips of banana on a baking sheet lined with greased baking parchment or waxed paper. Bake for about 1 hour in the preheated oven.

2 Remove from the oven, let cool, then peel the chips off the paper. Dust with the sugar and cinnamon, if desired, and serve with the yogurt.

    Preparation/cooking
2 minutes/1 hour

Oven temperature
225°F/110°C

 Makes 8 portions

 Nutritional information
Rich source of vitamin C.

JELL-O BOATS

2 large oranges, halved

4oz (125g) package fruit gelatin, e.g., strawberry or orange

1 small can mandarin orange segments (optional)

1 pint fresh raspberries (optional)

TO DECORATE

8 small rice paper triangles

8 party toothpicks

Of all the foods I make for parties, these ingeniously simple "boats" are perhaps the most popular.

1 Squeeze the juice from the oranges (keep it to drink) without breaking the skin. Carefully scrape out the membrane and discard.

2 Make the gelatin according to package instructions, reducing the amount of water specified by a quarter if using fruit. Divide the fruit, if using, between the orange halves, then fill with gelatin and refrigerate until set.

3 Take a wet knife and cut each orange half in half again. Thread a toothpick down the center of each rice paper triangle, then set it in the gelatin.

VARIATION

To make shaped gelatin, make the gelatin according to package instructions, using half the amount of water specified. Pour into a deep nonstick baking sheet and refrigerate until set. Cut into shapes using a wet knife (see page 105 for illustration).

Preparation/cooking
5 minutes/10 minutes, plus 1¾ hours setting

Makes 8 portions

— NOTE —

These boats use toothpicks. For young children, place the boats on each child's plate, and then remove the toothpicks.

18 Months - 2 Years

Food tastes are decided early in life, so you should try to establish a varied, healthy diet for your child while she is still receptive to new foods. However, despite your best efforts, your plans may be derailed by a period of faddy or erratic eating. You may have to use a little ingenuity to stimulate her appetite. This chapter is full of ideas for healthy "fast foods" that should encourage even the most reluctant child to try new foods.

The Active Toddler

TODDLERHOOD IS A TIME of growing individuality. Your child will have attained a much higher level of physical coordination, and she will be displaying her personality and temperament both verbally and physically. As your toddler works to establish her character, she may begin to exert an independent spirit at mealtimes. This may call for consistent but sensitive treatment.

Busy bodies

As your child nears her second birthday, her growth rate slows down substantially. At the same time, her levels of activity are on the increase because she has greater physical competence and probably a busier, more active daily schedule. Consequently, your rounded baby will become a slimmed-down, active toddler,

losing much of her "baby fat." Although she has high energy requirements, her small stomach will probably cope best with light meals interspersed with "energy" snacks. Remember that toddlers are not conditioned into eating by the clock, and, quite sensibly, will tend to want to eat only when they are truly hungry.

By this age they will be fairly vocal in their preferences and you will want to give your child easily prepared food that you can rustle up quickly before her hungry demands become furious outbursts (see pages 86-7). Of course, you will want to create some structure and routine for family mealtimes, but be flexible. The last thing you want to do is make an issue over "correct" mealtimes, turning your child into a resentful eater.

TANTRUMS

Remember that your child is entering the stage of toddler tantrums when the frustrations she encounters can lead her to explode with rage. This is hard for you too, and you may need to try out a number of ways to encourage her eating (see page 85). Avoid using bribes to get her to eat, however, as you will only encourage difficult behavior.

GAMES OR GRIPES?
Rejecting food can be a highly successful means of grabbing attention. It is often best just to remove the food rather than create an issue out of his behavior.

Snacks

Colorful and easy-to-handle snacks have wide appeal. An occasional treat of chocolate or chips will do no harm, but these foods offer only "empty" calories that provide instant but short-lived energy and shouldn't replace healthy snacks. Carbohydrates should be your child's main energy source. Starches, found in pasta, whole wheat bread, and cereals are excellent energizing foods since they release calories slowly and help keep energy levels constant. For simple, healthy snacks try:

- Chunky tomato & cream cheese dip (see page 88)
- Shaped sandwiches (see page 89)
- Pasta salad (see page 108)

PASTA SALAD
WITH VEGETABLE PIECES

WHOLE WHEAT
SANDWICHES

CREAMY DIP
WITH VEGETABLES

"GRAZING" HABITS

It is easy to misjudge exactly how much your child is eating, particularly if your family tends to snack rather than sit down for meals. If you are worried that your child's food intake is low, and that the amounts of food she consumes at mealtimes are frequently miniscule, try to keep a diary of her total food intake over a period of a few days, or even a week. Many children have the habit of "grazing" – taking a little food here and there. However, if all these snacks are added up over the period you have monitored, you may find that your child's diet is reasonably substantial and balanced.

Limiting sugary foods

As toddlers are exposed to an increasingly varied diet, they may be quick to acquire a "sweet tooth." Since they are most likely to pick up their eating habits from the immediate family, you may need to be disciplined yourself if you want your child to have a low sugar intake. It is not just the amount of sugar we eat that harms our teeth but also the frequency with which we put sugary foods in our mouth: each time we eat sugary foods, the bacteria in dental plaque produce acids that attack tooth enamel and can cause tooth decay. Consequently, a package of candy consumed all at once does less harm than eating it over a prolonged period of time. It is also much better to confine sugary foods to mealtimes because eating other foods at the same time dilutes the acid and reduces the harmful effects of the sugar. Moreover, at mealtimes there is more saliva in the mouth to wash away acids. Cheese is particularly beneficial at the end of a meal because it helps reduce acid saliva.

CANDY AS A REWARD

Do not let candy and desserts become synonymous with rewards: try to offer other treats, such as stickers or comics. Consider making a rule that candy is allowed only at certain times, even once a week, perhaps on Sundays.

SWEET DRINKS

Even pure fruit juices contain fructose (a natural sugar) which can cause tooth decay, so confine diluted fruit juices to mealtimes, where they can also benefit your child by increasing the absorption of iron from food. Read labels carefully; sugar can be disguised under other names such as glucose, maltose, or dextrose. Some individual cartons of fruit juice contain as much as 1oz (30g) of sugar. Diet soft drinks are no kinder to teeth – they too contain acids that attack tooth enamel. Sweet drinks at bedtime are not a good idea, since saliva won't wash away the acid during the night and you'll destroy any good work done by toothpaste.

The fussy eater

Refusing food is one of the first ways young children can flex their muscles and assert their drive for independence. It doesn't take them long to realize how easy it is to manipulate you at the dinner table. Indeed, battles at mealtimes are often one of the most stressful aspects of early parenthood. Cajoling a child to eat – whether in the form of bribery, threats, even the frantic production of a culinary masterpiece – is usually counter-productive.

KEEPING CALM

However unreasonable your child's eating habits seem to be, try to respond calmly. The aim is to help your child slide into normal family eating, not to force her into cooperation. Don't put pressure on your child to eat the foods you want her to eat. Try to keep the emotional temperature down: food shouldn't be used as a means to teach a child to do as she is told. It is an unfortunate fact of life that many children seem to enjoy stretching their parents' patience to the limit: after all, refusing to eat makes them the center of attention. The only way to counter this aspect of the problem is to refuse to be riled; simply take the rejected meal away. Attempting to induce guilt also won't work: don't make a child feel that she has a moral duty to leave a clean plate – it is unlikely to motivate a 2-year-old into finishing her dinner. It helps

to remember that no young child ever starves herself and that her fussy diet may well be nutritious, if unconventional. Rather than worry about your child's diet on a daily basis, remember that it is the balance of her diet over several days that really matters.

FADDY EATING

Occasionally children go through periods of eating only a few specific foods. If, for example, your child wants only peanut butter sandwiches at every meal, don't worry too much. Make sure the bread is whole wheat and maybe slip in some sliced banana or give her a milkshake or a glass of milk to accompany the sandwich. Continue to offer some tasty and nutritious alternatives. Children can thrive on quite a limited range of foods and, except in rare cases, will eventually get bored with a monotonous diet. Sometimes fads may be more pronounced, and appear even more irrational: your child might refuse foods that have come into contact with each other on her plate, for instance, so a sectioned plate may provide a solution to this temporary phase.

REJECTING SPECIFIC FOODS

If your child continually rejects a particular food, you can assume that she really doesn't like it. Sometimes it is best to respect your child's wishes: after all, adults have likes and dislikes. Try to recognize when your child is

USING CUTLERY
By 18 months your child may have the dexterity to use a spoon and fork. Letting her have her own cutlery and plate may make her a more enthusiastic eater.

being stubborn and when she has a genuine dislike of a particular food. If vegetables are a problem, there are many ways to disguise them in the diet (see page 65). Meat is another food that is often rejected. A healthy diet need not include meat, provided your child's diet includes milk and dairy products, beans and legumes, or soy-based products, which will provide adequate quantities of protein, iron, and B vitamins (see page 37). However, it is often the texture rather than the taste of meat that children object to. Your child may dislike lumps of meat, but dishes such as spaghetti bolognese (see page 61) or shepherd's pie (see page 77) may make meat more palatable, particularly if the meat is blended until fairly smooth. You could also make bite-size meatballs (see page 97) and serve them with ketchup, or chop meat very finely, moisten with gravy, and mix it into a combination of mashed potatoes and carrots.

More strategies

You may have to try several ways of encouraging your child to eat well. Respond creatively to some of her behavioral quirks, but don't cast all rules aside. Try to be the one who takes the initiative, rather than being ruled by your child: consistency is also important.

ALLOWING INDEPENDENCE

Give your child scope to assert her independence, perhaps by letting her choose two out of three vegetables offered to her. You can also involve her in food preparation or let her choose fruit when you go shopping. It is sensible to keep portions small and give second helpings if requested. Your child will then feel that she has control over how much she eats, and she won't be put off by a heaping plate.

SNACKING
Offer a few easily managed finger foods that can be eaten at leisure.

MAKE MEALTIMES SOCIABLE

Mealtimes are social occasions, so set a good example by eating with your child as often as possible, then encourage her to eat what you are enjoying (and avoid distractions like television). Inviting a friend over, adding a few appealing presentational touches, or changing the venue can work wonders.

REMEMBER

◆ AVOID EMPTY CALORIES, as in soft drinks or candy; keep a supply of healthy snacks on hand.

◆ IF YOU ARE really worried about how much and what your child is eating, keep a weekly record of her food intake. You will probably find that her diet is surprisingly well balanced.

◆ IF YOUR CHILD likes to play with her food before eating it, let her, and forget about perfecting table manners for the time being.

◆ PROVIDE SMALL SERVINGS, or make individual portions of food: they are less off-putting and allow your child some control over how much food she takes.

◆ CHANGE THE VENUE of meals occasionally: even a picnic lunch on the floor may work.

CHANGING THE VENUE
A teddy bear's picnic outdoors will make snack-time into a great treat.

Fast Foods for Toddlers

THE ACTIVE TODDLER'S HUNGER rarely coincides with
regular mealtimes. Because she uses up energy so quickly
with her newfound independence, light, frequent snacks
may best suit her needs. She is also too young to wait patiently for meals,
so it is a good idea to be able to offer easy-to-prepare, healthy "fast foods."
All the foods shown here are visually appealing and have interesting
textures and vibrant flavors – and all can be eaten "on the run."

*Cherry tomato
and tofu kabobs
(see page 92)*

*Carrot stars made
with a miniature
cookie cutter*

KABOBS IN PITA POCKETS
Miniature kabobs can be grilled, taken
off the skewers, and stuffed into warm
pita bread pockets with some colorful
greens. Chicken with tomato and
tofu with chunky vegetables are
delicious combinations. (See pages
92 and 96 for recipes.)

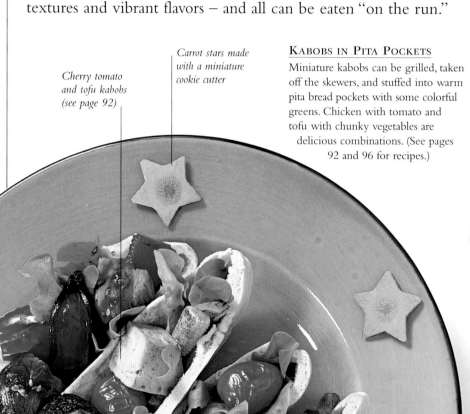

*Kabobs with
honey and
citrus marinade
(see page 89)*

CHUNKY TOMATO
& CREAM CHEESE DIP
Children often prefer vegetables
raw, especially if cut into whimsical
shapes, and they love dunking
them into dips. This makes a
nutritious between-meal snack.
(See page 88 for recipe.)

PINWHEEL SANDWICHES
Toddlers will adore
these sticky spirals of whole
wheat bread rolled with
their favorite fillings.
(See page 89 for recipe.)

MINI PIZZAS

English muffins simply split
in half and spread with
tomato sauce and cheese
and plenty of different
toppings make excellent
pizzas. Animal-face patterns
will be especially popular.
(See page 91 for recipe.)

Cheese and salad
double-deckers

Cheese and
chive kite

SHAPED
SANDWICHES

The most versatile
of fast foods, shaped
sandwiches make savory
mouthfuls. (See page 89 for recipes.)

SCRAMBLED EGGS WITH CHEESE & TOMATO

2 eggs

1 tbsp milk or light cream

salt and pepper, to taste

1 tbsp (15g) butter

1 tomato, peeled, seeded, and chopped

2 tbsp grated Gruyère cheese

Scrambled eggs make a quick and nutritious family breakfast. Serve them with a toasted bagel or buttered toast. For a special breakfast or brunch, add strips of smoked salmon.

1 Beat the eggs with the milk and season lightly. Melt the butter in a saucepan over low heat, add the chopped tomato, and sauté for 1 minute.

2 Add the egg mixture and heat, stirring constantly with a wooden spoon, until the eggs start to cook. Add the cheese and continue to stir until the eggs are set. Serve immediately.

 Preparation/cooking
2 minutes/6 minutes

 Makes 2 portions

 Nutritional information
Rich source of calcium, iron, protein, vitamin A, B vitamins, and vitamin E.

APPLE, MANGO & APRICOT MUESLI

¼ cup (45g) each chopped dried mango and apricots

2 tbsp (30g) golden raisins

¾ cup (125g) muesli base, or ½ cup (60g) each of oat and wheat flakes

¼ cup (30g) finely chopped hazelnuts (optional)

1½ cups (350ml) apple and mango juice or plain apple juice

½ red apple, cored and chopped

extra fresh fruit such as banana or raspberries (optional)

Unfortunately, many breakfast cereals designed for children are low in nutrients and high in sugar. I make a healthy, Swiss-style muesli for my family using a commercial muesli – a mixture of rolled oats, wheat, barley, and rye flakes – and fresh fruit. This mix, without the added fresh fruit, can be kept in the refrigerator for several days.

Mix the dried fruit, muesli, and nuts with the juice. Refrigerate and soak overnight or for several hours. In the morning, stir in the apple and your chosen extra fresh fruit.

VARIATION

Substitute grape juice for apple juice and use chopped dried peaches instead of mango and apricots.

 Preparation
5 minutes, plus overnight soaking

 Makes 4 portions

 Nutritional information
Rich source of fiber, folic acid, iron, protein, vitamin A, B vitamins, and zinc.

—— NOTE ——
This recipe contains nuts. Leave out if there is a family history of nut allergy.

CHUNKY TOMATO & CREAM CHEESE DIP

1 cup (200g) soft cream cheese

3 tbsp mayonnaise

1 tbsp ketchup

1 tsp fresh lemon juice

¼ tsp Worcestershire sauce

¼ tsp soy sauce

½ tbsp snipped fresh chives

2 tomatoes, peeled, seeded, and chopped

Serve this appealing dip with raw and cooked vegetables, bread soldiers, or pita toasts for a tasty and energizing snack.

Simply mix all the ingredients together, blending them thoroughly, and spoon into small bowls.

VARIATION

To make a cream cheese and chive dip, mix together the same quantities of soft cream cheese and mayonnaise with 3 tablespoons of milk. Mix in 1 teaspoon of Dijon mustard, 2 tablespoons of snipped fresh chives, a pinch of sugar, and freshly ground pepper to taste.

 Preparation
10 minutes

 Makes 8 portions

 Nutritional information
Rich source of vitamin A, vitamin B12, and vitamin E.

See page 86 for illustration.

—— TIP ——
This dip can also be made with low-fat dairy products, but only for older children.

SHAPED SANDWICHES

Sandwiches make a quick snack that can be eaten on the run. What's more, you can use all sorts of fillings and types of bread. Those that use foods from each of the main groups — bread, fruits and vegetables, meat and alternatives, dairy products — are a nutritious alternative to cooked meals.

EGG SALAD
CUT-OUT DUCKLING

CUCUMBER AND CHEESE
OPEN SANDWICH

EGG SALAD AND AVOCADO
DOUBLE-DECKER

SMOKED SALMON PINWHEEL

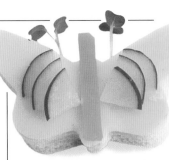

SALAD AND CHEESE
CUT-OUT BUTTERFLY

CHEESE AND RED PEPPER
OPEN SANDWICH

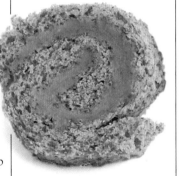

WHOLE WHEAT PINWHEEL
WITH SPINACH PÂTÉ

PITA BREAD POCKET

OPEN SANDWICHES

Cut slices of bread into simple shapes or animal shapes using cookie cutters. Butter and then spread with filling. Try cottage cheese or mashed egg sheep or ducks; geometric shapes spread with a favorite filling, such as diamond-shaped bread kites spread with mashed avocado, or with thinly sliced ham or chicken; or bread and cheese squares decorated to look like packages with sweet pepper or chive ribbons. (See pages 87 and 104 for additional illustrations.)

DOUBLE-DECKER SANDWICHES

Take 3 slices of buttered whole wheat or white bread, with the center slice buttered on both sides. Sandwich together with 2 complementary but contrasting fillings, such as sliced banana and strawberry jam; grated cheese and shredded lettuce with finely sliced ham; or mashed avocado and egg salad. Cut into strips. (See page 87 for additional illustrations.)

PINWHEEL SANDWICHES

Trim the crusts off 2 thin slices of bread. Overlap the edges slightly and flatten with a rolling pin so that they join together. Butter and spread with a colorful filling and roll up, jelly-roll fashion. Cut across into thin rounds. Suggested fillings: peanut butter and jam; cream cheese and mashed avocado; egg salad with watercress. (See page 87 for additional illustrations.)

MINI PITA BREAD POCKETS

Warm a small pita bread, cut in half, and fill with a savory mix; for example, grated cheese or shredded chicken or ham with salad; sliced hard-boiled egg with lettuce; or mashed sardines and sliced tomato.

ALPHABET PASTA MINESTRONE

2 tbsp vegetable oil

1 onion, finely chopped

1 cup (125g) diced carrots

½ celery stalk, finely chopped

¼ cup (30g) finely chopped
leeks, white parts only

¼lb (125g) potatoes, chopped

½ cup (60g) diced zucchini

2 tomatoes, peeled,
seeded, and chopped

7½ cups (1½ liters) chicken
stock (see page 46)

2 tsp tomato paste

½ cup (60g) frozen peas

½ cup (45g) alphabet pasta

salt and pepper, to taste

Homemade minestrone makes a nutritious soup for children and also becomes a satisfying family meal if accompanied by bread and salad. You can add shredded cabbage (about 4oz/125g) to make it even more substantial, if desired. The tiny alphabet pasta shapes appeal to children.

1 Heat the oil in a large pan, add the onion, and sauté for about 5 minutes. Add the carrots, celery, and leeks, and sauté until they begin to soften, about 5 minutes. Add the potatoes and zucchini and sauté for 2–3 minutes.

2 Stir in the chopped tomatoes, stock, and tomato paste. Bring to a boil, then cover and simmer for 20 minutes. Add the frozen peas, return the soup to a boil, and cook for 5 minutes.

3 Stir in the alphabet pasta, return the soup to a boil, then simmer for about 5 minutes longer. Taste and season lightly.

 Preparation/cooking
10 minutes/45 minutes

 Makes 8 portions

 Nutritional information
Rich source of beta-carotene, fiber, folic acid, vitamin A, and vitamin C.

 Suitable for freezing

—— TIP ——
This soup can also be made with vegetable stock.

BOW-TIE PASTA WITH SPRING VEGETABLES

4oz (125g) pasta
bows (farfalle)

2 tbsp (30g) butter

¼ cup (30g) finely chopped leeks

½ cup (60g) diced carrots

½ cup (60g) diced zucchini

½ cup (60g) small broccoli
florets

salt and pepper, to taste

⅔ cup (150ml) light cream

¼ cup (30g) freshly grated
Parmesan

This is simple to prepare, but never fails to please. You can use other pasta shapes such as tagliatelle or penne with the creamy sauce.

1 Bring a pot of lightly salted water to a boil, add the pasta, and cook until tender, about 10 minutes, or according to package instructions.

2 Meanwhile, melt the butter in a heavy-bottomed saucepan, add the leeks and carrots, and sauté for about 5 minutes. Add the zucchini and broccoli and cook for about 7 minutes, or until all the vegetables are tender. Season to taste.

3 Pour in the cream and cook, stirring, for 1 minute. Remove from the heat and stir in the Parmesan. Toss the pasta with the sauce, and serve.

 Preparation/cooking
10 minutes/20 minutes

 Makes 4 portions

 Nutritional information
Rich source of beta-carotene, calcium, fiber, folic acid, protein, vitamin B12, vitamin C, and zinc.

 Suitable for freezing
sauce only

Use mushroom slices, uncooked cheese, and black olives for the eyes and nose

Corn kernel teeth

DECORATED MINI PIZZAS
Quirkily decorated small pizzas have instant child appeal. Older children can make their own toppings using a selection of prepared ingredients.

MOUSE FACE PIZZA
Use steamed zucchini pieces for ears, stuffed olive slices for eyes, a black olive for the nose, and strips of carrot for whiskers.

MINI PIZZAS

Adding a selection of colorful vegetables to mini pizzas is a great way to encourage your child to eat more vegetables. For a special occasion, you might like to make animal face designs, as shown above.

2 muffins, split in half, or 1 small baguette, cut in half

4 tbsp good tomato sauce (homemade or bought)

½ cup (60g) grated Cheddar, Gruyère, or mozzarella cheese

ADDITIONAL TOPPING

1 tbsp (15g) butter

1 tbsp chopped scallions

½ cup (60g) thinly sliced zucchini

¾ cup (60g) mushrooms, sliced

salt and pepper, to taste

corn kernels, raw pepper strips, cheese shapes, olives, and fresh basil leaves (optional)

1 To make the topping, heat the butter in a pan, add the scallions, and sauté for 1 minute. Add the zucchini and mushrooms and sauté until just tender, about 4 minutes. Season to taste.

2 Lightly toast the muffins or baguette. Divide the tomato sauce between each of the cut sides of muffin or baguette, spread evenly, then sprinkle with cheese. Top with cooked vegetables, perhaps making patterns or animal faces, then cook under a preheated broiler until the cheese is bubbling and golden. If desired, use the corn, uncooked pepper, cheese, olives, and basil to decorate further.

Preparation/cooking
10 minutes/15 minutes

Makes 4 portions

Nutritional information
Rich source of calcium, protein, vitamin A, and B vitamins.

See page 87 for additional illustration.

CORN, CHERRY TOMATO & TOFU KABOBS

9oz (275g) firm tofu, cubed

6 baby corn, halved

1 zucchini, trimmed and sliced into round chunks

8 cherry tomatoes

4 mini pitas, split in half

salad greens, to garnish

MARINADE

1½ tbsp soy sauce

1½ tbsp honey

1½ tbsp Chinese plum sauce

1 tbsp vegetable oil

1 scallion, finely chopped

Tofu (bean curd) is a nutritious alternative to meat. Although naturally bland, it is delicious marinated for it soaks up flavors well, and its soft texture appeals to children.

1 Combine the ingredients for the marinade in a small cup. Put the tofu in a shallow bowl and pour the marinade over it. Cover and let it soak for about 1 hour. While the tofu marinates, soak 4 wooden skewers in cold water.

2 Thread alternate pieces of tofu, corn, zucchini, and tomatoes on the skewers. Brush with some of the marinade. Cook the kabobs under a hot broiler or on the grill, basting occasionally, for about 3 minutes on each side, or until the vegetables are tender and the tofu is nicely browned.

3 Slide the kabobs off the skewers, arrange in the pita pockets, and garnish with the greens.

Preparation/cooking
1 hour 5 minutes, incl.
1 hour marinating/
6 minutes

Makes 4 portions

Nutritional information
Rich source of calcium, fiber, folic acid, iron, protein, vitamin A, vitamin C, vitamin E, and zinc.

See page 86 for main illustration.

TIP
The corn and zucchini may be parboiled before skewering, if preferred.

MULTICOLORED RICE WITH KIDNEY BEANS

1 tbsp olive oil

½ onion, chopped

1 garlic clove, crushed

¼ cup (30g) each seeded and chopped red and green pepper

¼ cup (30g) diced carrots

½ cup (125g) long-grain white rice

1¼ cups (300ml) chicken stock (see page 46) or vegetable stock

1 tomato, peeled, seeded, and chopped

⅓ cup (45g) frozen peas

2oz (60g) canned red kidney beans

Combining kidney beans with rice creates a high-quality protein dish for children who don't like meat. The bright colors are very appealing.

1 Heat the oil in a skillet. Add the onion and garlic and sauté until softened. Add the peppers and carrots, and sauté for 2 minutes, stirring occasionally. Stir in the rice and cook for 2–3 minutes.

2 Pour in the chicken stock, add the chopped tomato, and bring the mixture to a boil. Reduce the heat, cover, and simmer for 10 minutes.

3 Remove the cover, add the peas and beans, and cook, stirring occasionally, for 6 minutes, or until the rice and vegetables are tender.

VARIATION
Omit the kidney beans and add ½ cup (75g) each diced ham and canned or frozen corn.

Preparation/cooking
5 minutes/25 minutes

Makes 4 portions

Nutritional information
Rich source of beta-carotene, fiber, folic acid, protein, vitamin C, and zinc.

Sweet & Sour Vegetable Stir-Fry

1½ tbsp vegetable oil

1 onion, cut into rings

2oz (60g) baby corn, cut into quarters

½ cup (60g) thinly sliced carrots, cut into shapes with a tiny cookie cutter

1 cup (90g) broccoli, cut into small florets

¼ cup (90g) bean sprouts

½ small red pepper, cored, seeded, and cut into strips

1 scallion, finely chopped

pinch of black pepper

Sweet & Sour Sauce

⅔ cup (150ml) vegetable stock

½ tbsp cornstarch blended with 1 tbsp cold water

2 tsp brown sugar

½ tbsp soy sauce

One of the best ways to encourage your child to eat vegetables is to make a colorful stir-fry. It's important to make sure that the vegetables remain crisp to retain their flavor and nutrients.

1 Heat the oil in a wok or skillet. Add the onion and sauté until softened, about 5 minutes. Add the corn, carrots, and broccoli florets, and stir-fry for 2 minutes.

2 Add the bean sprouts, red pepper, and scallion and stir-fry for 2 minutes longer. Season with a little black pepper.

3 To make the sauce, blend the vegetable stock with the cornstarch paste in a small pan. Mix in the brown sugar and soy sauce. Set over high heat, bring to a boil, and simmer for about 2 minutes, until the sauce is thickened. Toss the hot vegetables with the sauce and heat through in the wok.

Preparation/cooking
15 minutes/15 minutes

Makes 4 portions

Nutritional information
Rich source of beta-carotene, fiber, folic acid, iron, and vitamin C.

— Tip —
For young children, blanch the carrots and broccoli first to make them softer to chew.

VEGETARIAN CROQUETTES

3 medium potatoes, peeled and roughly chopped

1 tbsp (15g) butter

salt and pepper, to taste

¼ cup (75g) broccoli, cut into small florets

½ cup (60g) chopped carrots

⅓ cup (45g) frozen corn

2oz (60g) Cheddar cheese

salted potato chips, crushed

1 Bring a large pot of lightly salted water to a boil, add the potatoes, and cook until tender. Drain and mash with the butter and seasoning.

2 Meanwhile, place the vegetables in a steamer and cook until tender, 6–7 minutes. Mix with the mashed potatoes and season to taste.

3 Cut the cheese into 8 sticks. Use your hands to shape the potato and vegetable mixture around the cheese to form 8 sausage-shaped croquettes.

4 Roll the croquettes in the crushed chips until well coated and place on a baking sheet. Bake in the preheated oven for 15 minutes.

 Preparation/cooking
10 minutes/40 minutes

 Oven temperature
350°F/180°C

 Makes 8 portions

 Nutritional information
Rich source of beta-carotene, calcium, fiber, folic acid, protein, vitamin B12, and vitamin C.

 Suitable for freezing

ANNABEL'S VEGETABLE CROQUETTES

½lb (200g) sweet potatoes

¼lb (100g) butternut squash

1 medium potato

½ cup (75g) finely chopped leeks, white part only

2 cups (150g) chopped mushrooms

2 tbsp chopped fresh parsley

2 cups (125g) bread crumbs

½ tbsp soy sauce

½ lightly beaten egg

salt and pepper, to taste

flour for coating

vegetable oil for frying

These are good eaten hot or cold and would be ideal for a lunch box or picnic.

1 Peel and grate the sweet potato, squash, and potato. Using your hands, squeeze out some of the excess moisture from the grated pulp.

2 In a mixing bowl, combine all the vegetables with the parsley, bread crumbs, soy sauce, and beaten egg. Season to taste.

3 Form the mixture into about 12 walnut-size croquettes. Spread the flour on a plate and coat the croquettes lightly.

4 Heat the oil in a large skillet, add the croquettes, and sauté over medium heat for 8–10 minutes, turning occasionally, until golden on the outside and cooked through.

 Preparation/cooking
25 minutes/10 minutes

 Oven temperature
350°F/180°C

 Makes 4 portions

 Nutritional information
Rich source of beta-carotene, calcium, fiber, iron, B vitamins, vitamin C, and vitamin E.

Suitable for freezing

— TIP —
This recipe is best made with fresh white bread crumbs, but you could use whole wheat bread crumbs instead.

SALMON STARFISH

1lb (500g) potatoes, cooked and cooled

2 tbsp ketchup

1 tsp Worcestershire sauce

1 lightly beaten egg

2 tbsp chopped fresh chives

¾lb (375g) cooked salmon fillets, flaked

3 tbsp fresh bread crumbs, plus extra for coating

a little melted butter

I serve these with shredded green bean "seaweed" and Special Tomato Sauce (see page 122).

1 Mash the potatoes with the ketchup, Worcestershire sauce, egg, and chives. Mix in the salmon and 3 tablespoons of bread crumbs. Shape the mixture into flat patties.

2 Use a large star-shaped cookie cutter to cut 8 starfish shapes. Gently pull out the points of the stars. Coat with bread crumbs and brush with butter.

3 Set the fish cakes on a lightly greased baking sheet. Transfer to the preheated oven and cook for 4 minutes on each side.

 Preparation/cooking
20 minutes/8 minutes

 Oven temperature
350°F/180°C

 Makes 8 portions

 Nutritional information
Rich source of folic acid, protein, B vitamins, and vitamin D.

 Suitable for freezing

——— TIP ———
These fish cakes can be shallow-fried instead of oven-baked.

MINI GOLDEN FISH BALLS

4 tbsp vegetable oil

1 tbsp (15g) butter

1 onion, finely chopped

1lb (500g) finely chopped fish, such as haddock, bream, whiting, cod, or hake

2oz (60g) carrots, finely grated

1 tbsp chopped fresh parsley

1 tbsp superfine sugar

½ lightly beaten egg

1 tbsp flour

salt and pepper, to taste

These are just the right size for toddlers to pick up. They are not at all fishy and have an appealing, slightly sweet taste. My fishmonger prepares a mixture of ground fish, but you could make your own mixture in a food processor.

1 Heat a tablespoon of vegetable oil and the butter in a small skillet. Add the onion and sauté for about 5 minutes, or until just softened.

2 Put the fish in a bowl and stir in the onion, carrots, parsley, sugar, beaten egg, and flour. Season to taste, then form the mixture into about 24 balls about the size of a large cherry tomato.

3 Heat the remaining 3 tablespoons of vegetable oil in the skillet. Add the fish balls and cook for about 10 minutes, until golden brown all over. Drain on paper towels.

 Preparation/cooking
5 minutes/20 minutes

 Makes 8 portions

 Nutritional information
Rich source of protein, vitamin A, vitamin B12, and vitamin E.

 Suitable for freezing

ONE-POT RICE WITH CHICKEN

2 tbsp olive oil

1 onion, finely chopped

½ cup (60g) diced carrots

1 tbsp chopped fresh parsley

¼lb (125g) chicken breast, diced

1 cup (175g) basmati rice, rinsed

1½ cups (350ml) chicken stock (see page 46)

1 cup (200g) canned chopped tomatoes

½ cup (60g) frozen peas

2 tbsp freshly grated Parmesan

This rice dish is easy to make and delicious. You can omit the chicken and add extra vegetables, if you like.

1 Heat the oil in a pan. Add the onion and sauté until softened. Add the carrots and parsley and sauté for 2–3 minutes. Add the chicken and cook for 2–3 minutes.

2 Add the rice to the pan and stir for 1 minute. Pour in the chicken stock and stir in the tomatoes and peas. Bring the mixture to a boil, then cover and simmer for 15 minutes.

3 Remove the cover and cook, stirring occasionally, for 5 minutes, or until the rice is tender. Remove from the heat and stir in the Parmesan.

 Preparation/cooking
5 minutes/30 minutes

 Makes 8 portions

 Nutritional information
Rich source of beta-carotene, calcium, folic acid, protein, and zinc.

 Suitable for freezing

CRUNCHY CHICKEN FINGERS

salt and pepper, to taste

¼ cup (30g) flour

1 chicken breast, cut into 6 strips

1 small egg, lightly beaten

1 cup (45g) cornflakes, crushed with a rolling pin

2 tbsp vegetable oil

These crunchy chicken pieces make a tasty finger food. Serve them with a little bowl of ketchup.

1 Lightly season the flour and put into a plastic bag. Add the chicken pieces and shake until coated.

2 Dip the chicken fingers in beaten egg, then roll them in the cornflakes. Heat the oil in a skillet, add the chicken, and sauté for about 6 minutes on each side, or until crunchy on the outside and cooked through.

 Preparation/cooking
5 minutes/13 minutes

 Makes 2 portions

 Nutritional information
Rich source of folic acid, iron, protein, and B vitamins.

Suitable for freezing
before cooking

CHICKEN KABOBS WITH HONEY & CITRUS MARINADE

1 boneless chicken breast and 4 thighs, skinned and trimmed

½ red pepper, cut into chunks

½ small onion, cut into chunks

4 mini pitas, split in half

salad leaves, to garnish

MARINADE

1 tbsp soy sauce

1 tbsp honey

1 tbsp each freshly squeezed lemon juice and orange juice

1 tsp vegetable oil

Use your own choice of vegetables for these tasty kabobs, perhaps mushrooms or zucchini.

1 Combine the marinade ingredients in a bowl. Cut the chicken into small chunks and add to the marinade with the pepper and onion. Cover and marinate for at least 30 minutes. Meanwhile, soak 4 wooden skewers in cold water.

2 Thread alternate pieces of chicken, pepper, and onion onto the skewers. Transfer to a hot broiler or barbecue grill and cook for about 5 minutes on each side, or until cooked through and browned.

3 Slide the kabobs off the skewers, arrange alternate pieces of chicken and vegetable in the pita bread pockets, and garnish with greens.

 Preparation/cooking
35 minutes/10 minutes

 Makes 4 portions

 Nutritional information
Rich source of beta-carotene, folic acid, iron, protein, B vitamins, vitamin C, and zinc.

See page 86 for illustration.

─── TIP ───
Add ½ tablespoon of sesame seeds to the marinade for extra flavor, if desired.

CHICKEN BOLOGNESE

2 tbsp vegetable oil

1 shallot, finely chopped

1 garlic clove, crushed

1 leek, trimmed and sliced

1lb (500g) ground chicken

1 carrot, diced

1½ cups (400g) canned chopped tomatoes

½ cup (125ml) water

1 tsp superfine sugar

2 tsp ketchup

2 tsp fresh thyme leaves

salt and pepper, to taste

You can use ground chicken or turkey to make a delicious pasta sauce. This version would make a good cannelloni filling. If you don't have fresh thyme, substitute ½ teaspoon of dried thyme.

1 Heat the vegetable oil in a skillet, add the shallot and garlic, and sauté over low heat for 2–3 minutes. Add the leek and sauté for about 3 minutes, until beginning to soften.

2 Add the chicken, breaking it up with a fork so that it does not stick together, and sauté for about 3 minutes. Add the carrot and then stir in the remaining ingredients.

3 Bring the mixture to a boil and then simmer for about 20 minutes, stirring occasionally, until the vegetables are tender and the chicken is cooked through. Season lightly and serve with pasta.

 Preparation/cooking
5 minutes/30 minutes

 Makes 8 portions

 Nutritional information
Rich source of beta–carotene, folic acid, protein, B vitamins, and zinc.

 Suitable for freezing

LAMB MEATBALLS WITH A SWEET & SOUR SAUCE

MEATBALLS

½lb (250g) ground lamb

1 onion, finely chopped

½ red pepper, finely chopped

1 tbsp finely chopped fresh parsley

1 small apple, peeled and grated

salt and pepper, to taste

flour for coating

2 tbsp vegetable oil for frying

SWEET & SOUR SAUCE

1½ cups (400g) canned chopped tomatoes

1 tbsp malt vinegar

1 tbsp brown sugar

1 tbsp ketchup

dash of Worcestershire sauce

These light and succulent meatballs in a tangy tomato-based sauce are delicious served with rice or pasta. They also make a good finger food served plain.

1 Mix together all the ingredients for the meatballs, seasoning to taste, then form the mixture into about 16 small balls. Spread the flour on a plate and coat the meatballs on all sides.

2 Heat the vegetable oil in a skillet, then add the meatballs and sauté for 10–15 minutes, turning them occasionally, until browned and almost cooked through.

3 Meanwhile, mix all the ingredients for the sauce together in a small pot set over medium–high heat and cook for 4 minutes. Taste and season, if necessary.

4 Pour the sauce over the meatballs in the skillet and cook over medium heat for about 10 minutes, or until the sauce has thickened and the meatballs are cooked through.

 Preparation/cooking
20 minutes/25 minutes

 Makes 8 portions

 Nutritional information
Rich source of folic acid, iron, protein, B vitamins, incl. B12, and zinc.

 Suitable for freezing

RAISIN & OATMEAL COOKIES

7 tbsp (100g) unsalted butter

⅓ cup (90g) granulated sugar

⅓ cup (90g) light brown sugar

1 egg

1 tsp vanilla extract

1 cup (125g) flour

½ tsp cinnamon

½ tsp baking powder

½ tsp baking soda

¼ tsp salt

½ cup (75g) rolled oats

1 cup (175g) raisins

1 Cream the butter and sugars together in an electric mixer, or by hand. Beat in the egg and vanilla extract.

2 Sift together the flour, cinnamon, baking powder, baking soda, and salt. Add to the mixture and beat until just combined. Stir in the oats and raisins.

3 Lightly grease 2 baking sheets. Using your hands, form the dough into about 22 walnut-size balls. Put them on the baking sheets, widely spaced, and flatten them down a little.

4 Transfer the cookies to the preheated oven and bake for about 10 minutes, or until lightly golden all over. Transfer to a wire rack and let cool. Store in an airtight container.

 Preparation/cooking 20 minutes/10 minutes

 Oven temperature 375°F/190°C

 Makes 22 cookies

 Suitable for freezing

BANANA MUFFINS

2 cups (60g) bran flakes

1¼ cups (300ml) milk

1 cup (125g) whole wheat flour

½ tsp salt

1 tbsp baking powder

4 tbsp (60g) butter

¼ cup (60g) superfine sugar

1 egg

2 bananas, mashed

½ cup (90g) raisins

These muffins are full of good natural ingredients, and they make a great breakfast food that can be eaten "on the run."

1 Soak the bran flakes in the milk for 10 minutes. Sift together the flour, salt, and baking powder.

2 Cream the butter and sugar, then beat in the egg. Stir in alternate spoonfuls of the soaked bran flakes and the flour mixture. Gently fold in the mashed bananas and the raisins.

3 Line a muffin tin with fluted paper cups and half fill each with the mixture. Bake in the preheated oven for 30 minutes.

 Preparation/cooking 15 minutes/30 minutes

 Oven temperature 350°F/180°C

 Makes 12 muffins

 Nutritional information Rich source of fiber, folic acid, iron, and B vitamins, incl. B12.

 Suitable for freezing

STRAWBERRY & BANANA SMOOTHIE

½ pint (125g) strawberries

1 small banana, cut into chunks

½ cup (140g) vanilla yogurt

4 tbsp milk, plus extra as necessary

Fruit and yogurt smoothies make tasty and nutritious drinks. For a special treat, substitute vanilla ice cream for the yogurt.

Process all the ingredients with a hand-held blender until smooth. Add extra milk to thin, if necessary.

VARIATION

Mix 2 tablespoons of hot milk with 3 tablespoons of instant malt powder. Add ⅔ cup (150ml) cold milk, 2 scoops of chocolate ice cream, and 2 broken-up chocolate cookies (optional). Blend until smooth.

 Preparation 5 minutes

 Makes 2 portions

 Nutritional information Rich source of calcium, folic acid, protein, vitamin B12, and vitamin C.

—— TIP ——
If the strawberries are not very sweet, you can add a little sugar or honey.

THREE-TIER
ICE POP

SUMMER FRUITS
ICE POP

ORANGE, PINEAPPLE,
AND PASSIONFRUIT
ICE POP

HOMEMADE ICE POPS

*8oz (250g) fresh or frozen
summer fruits (such as
strawberries, raspberries,
blueberries, pitted cherries,
or blackberries)*

2 tbsp confectioners' sugar, sieved

*⅔ cup (150ml) low-sugar
grape drink*

*1¼ cups (300g) raspberry or
strawberry yogurt*

*2 cups (500ml) fresh fruit
juice (such as orange
or pineapple)*

*There is one food that children are almost
guaranteed to like – ice pops. These pops
are made with ingredients that are actually good for
your child: pureed fruits, yogurt, and fresh fruit
juices. A three-tier pop looks great,
but you can use a single fruit flavor
with the juice of your choice.*

1 Put the summer fruits in a pot with the sugar and
cook over low heat for a few minutes, until soft
and mushy. Puree in a blender, stir in the grape drink,
then strain through a sieve. Set aside to cool.

2 Pour the mixture into 10–12 pop molds, filling
them about a third full, and freeze. When the first
layer is set, pour in yogurt to a depth of 1in (2.5cm)
and freeze. Once this layer is frozen, pour in the fresh
juice almost to the top, and place the cover with its
stick over each pop. Freeze again.

3 When ready to eat, run the mold under hot
water for a few seconds to loosen the pops.

VARIATION

Put a strawberry slice into each of 12 molds. Mix
3¾ cups (900ml) strained freshly squeezed orange
juice with 1½ cups (350ml) pineapple juice or exotic
fruit juice. Add the strained juice of 6 passionfruit.
Pour into the molds, cover, and freeze.

 Preparation
3–4 hours, incl.
freezing time

 Makes 12 pops
(or 10 if using
larger molds)

 Nutritional information
Rich source of vitamin C.

— TIP —
Adding a slice of fruit or a fresh
raspberry before pouring in the
juice can look very attractive.

2-3
Years

By the time your child reaches his second birthday, he should be joining in regularly in family meals and continuing to broaden his tastes. This is an excellent time to encourage an active interest in food, perhaps by allowing him to participate in fun, simple cooking tasks, or to help choose favorite dishes for a birthday party with friends.

Early Childhood

CHILDREN IN THIS AGE GROUP are often highly appreciative of their food, especially when it has the lively presentation of a party spread. It is surprising just how quiet a group of 2 to 3 year olds can be around a table laden with edible goodies. Others are more erratic and selective. Whatever his eating habits, your child will spend a lot of time with you in the kitchen and will enjoy joining in with your cooking activities.

Eating for an active day

Two and three year olds are highly active and often appear, if not thin, at least leggy. Your child will still need frequent small meals to meet his high energy requirements and there may be times when he seems in need of a rapid energy "fix" to stop him from becoming overtired or grumpy. Sugar and carbohydrates from refined sources (such as fizzy drinks or chocolate cookies) are quickly broken down into glucose and provide an instant "pick-me-up," but fruit or fruit juice is a healthier energy source that is also fast-working. Unrefined carbohydrate foods, such as bread, potatoes, or homemade cookies (see page 98) take longer to break down into glucose, but provide a more sustained energy supply.

"ENERGY" FOODS

FOR A QUICK SPURT OF ENERGY:
- Bowl of cornflakes
- Pieces of fruit, fresh or dried
- Yogurt with honey

FOR A STEADY STREAM OF ENERGY:
- Raw vegetables with dips
- Bread with ham, tuna, or cheese
- Potato skins with filling
- Baked beans on toast
- Salad with hard-boiled egg
- Oatcakes or rice cakes with cheese
- Freshly made fruit milkshakes

Cooking: a new activity

You can encourage your child's interest in food by involving him in its preparation early on. Children often take great pride in helping set the table, knead dough, or mix ingredients, and can be fascinated by quite ordinary tasks that adults take for granted: just think how many ways there are to prepare an egg, or how ingredients change shape, texture, and color if heated or frozen.

All this is a new experience for your child. Provided you keep him away from sharp knives or electrical equipment, there are plenty of supervised activities he can take part in, from breaking eggs into a bowl to cutting out cookies with cookie cutters. There are simple recipes in this book that would be ideal for your child to help you make. Try Mini Pizzas (page 91), Cheesy Bread Animals (page 106), Character Cakes (page 114), Shortbread Cookies (page 115), or Chewy Apricot & Cereal Bars (page 130).

LEARNING NEW SKILLS
Some of the messiest activities will be the most enjoyable. Let your child feel free to experiment.

Making mealtimes work

By the age of 2 your child will be able to sit on a secured booster seat at the table with you, and he will be eating very much what the rest of the family eats, although perhaps at different times. It is important, however, to keep him company at mealtimes if he is having his dinner before the rest of the family. Letting him sit alone at the table, even if you are in the same room, is bound to lead to trouble as he fights for your attention. Try to encourage his

enjoyment of food: include him in the family's lunch or evening meal as often as possible. Don't feel obliged to make novelty foods all the time, but do think about giving everyday meals some quick "child appeal." Without spending more than a few moments, a simple plate of food can be made to appeal to a child's sense of form and color; fresh fruit arranged in a pattern on his plate will bring a smile to his face and stimulate his interest.

"MOCK FRIED EGG"
Vanilla yogurt with half an apricot on top becomes a simple visual joke.

SAVORY DIP
A colorful array of vegetable and bread sticks has instant appeal.

SHEPHERD'S PIE
Make a mini portion in a ramekin and let your child decorate it as he wishes.

OBESITY

The most common nutritional disorder in the western world is obesity. Research suggests that childhood obesity may be related to adult obesity and that this association becomes stronger as childhood progresses. Obesity is a problem that tends to run in families, although a hereditary link has not been proved. However, by adopting a long-term approach to healthy eating, it should be possible to insure that your child's weight keeps pace with his increasing

height. If a child is already obviously overweight, most medical experts would encourage parents to adopt a healthier eating pattern as a family, rather than cut down on the amount of food offered. No child should ever go hungry, but if 99 percent of the diet consists of carbohydrates from starchy and cereal sources, fruits and vegetables, low-fat dairy foods, and fish or lean meat, then sugary, fatty, and processed foods are edged out and become a minimal part of the diet.

Most babies do go through a chubby stage, especially before they learn to walk, and this is perfectly natural and healthy. Chubbiness tends to disappear as children become more active; indeed improved levels of physical activity are a key factor in controlling obesity. Even a walk to the store or a game of catch in the park will help use up energy, improve muscle tone, and build strong bones. A purely weight-loss diet should not be an option for growing children.

Party Time

HERE ARE PARTY DISHES that look and taste wonderful. You can plan the party around a theme, perhaps serving foods with different distinctive shapes, as shown here, or choosing a color scheme. Don't provide only sweet foods: the healthier savory dishes can look just as good, but do serve them before you bring out the sweet things.

OPEN SANDWICHES

Daintily cut open sandwiches make easy finger foods for small children. These sandwiches are spread with butter or cream cheese, then topped with rounds of cucumber or tomato, squares of mild cheese or ham, or rosettes of smoked turkey.
(See page 89 for recipe.)

ANNABEL'S PASTA SALAD

A dish of multicolored pasta with plenty of vegetable chunks and a lively dressing should appeal to both small children and any accompanying parents. (See page 108 for recipe.)

Use cookie cutters to shape these nuggets

SHORTBREAD COOKIES & SHAPED JELL-O

These iced cookies can be made well ahead and in any shape. The Jell-o jubes in the center continue the star theme. (See pages 115 and 79 for recipes.)

A flower design is made with balls of icing

PACKAGE CAKE

A bold and bright birthday sponge cake shaped to look like a package makes a superb centerpiece. (See page 115 for recipe.)

HEART-SHAPED CHICKEN NUGGETS

These chicken and apple patties, with their moist inside and crunchy coating, will be an instant hit with children.
(See page 110 for recipe.)

TOMATO SOUP

1 tbsp olive oil

1 garlic clove, crushed

1 onion, chopped

½ cup (75g) diced carrots

1½ cups (400g) canned chopped tomatoes or 8 fresh tomatoes

1 tbsp tomato paste

2½ cups (600ml) vegetable stock

2 slices white bread, shredded

salt and pepper, to taste

pinch of sugar

2 tbsp torn fresh basil leaves

A really good homemade tomato soup is usually a great favorite with children. I prefer to use canned tomatoes since so many fresh tomatoes lack flavor, but if you have ripe, full-flavored, medium-size tomatoes, you can use them instead.

1 Heat the olive oil in a large pan over low heat, then add the garlic, onion, and carrots and sauté for 10 minutes, stirring occasionally.

2 Add the remaining ingredients except for the basil. Simmer for 10 minutes, stirring occasionally, until all the vegetables are soft.

3 Stir in the basil and simmer for 5 minutes longer. Puree until smooth in a blender.

 Preparation/cooking
10 minutes/26 minutes

 Makes 8 portions

Nutritional information
Rich source of beta-carotene and folic acid.

❄ Suitable for freezing

CHEESY BREAD ANIMALS

2 cups (250g) unbleached flour, plus flour to dust

pinch of salt

½ tbsp (½ package) fast-acting dried yeast

½ tsp honey

pinch of cayenne

1 tsp dry mustard

⅔ cup (approximately 150ml) warm water

½ cup (60g) grated aged Cheddar cheese

2 tbsp freshly grated Parmesan

TO DECORATE

1 egg, beaten

raisins

sesame seeds

poppy seeds

grated Cheddar cheese

Children adore making bread – it's a bit like playing with play dough – and they will have great fun forming this delicious cheesy bread into animal shapes.

1 Sift the flour and salt into a mixing bowl. Stir in the yeast, honey, cayenne, and mustard and just enough of the water to form a soft dough.

2 Transfer to a floured surface and knead lightly for about 5 minutes to make a smooth, pliable dough. Gradually knead the grated cheeses into the dough (this will produce a slightly streaky effect).

3 Shape the dough into 6 animal figures and transfer to a floured baking sheet. Cover them loosely with a dish towel and let rise in a warm place for about 1 hour, or until doubled in size.

4 Brush with beaten egg and add raisins for eyes. Sprinkle the tops with sesame seeds, poppy seeds, or grated cheese. Bake in the preheated oven for 20 minutes, or until golden brown. The undersides should sound hollow when tapped. Let the animals cool on a wire rack.

VARIATION

To make cheese and onion rolls, add 1 tablespoon of finely chopped scallions to the dough at the end of step 2.

 Preparation/cooking
1½ hours, incl. 1 hour rising/20 minutes

 Oven temperature
400°F/200°C

 Makes 6 rolls

 Nutritional information
Rich source of calcium, folic acid, protein, vitamin B12, and zinc.

❄ Suitable for freezing

TUNA &
CORN FILLING

CRANBERRY &
TURKEY FILLING

BARBECUE
BEAN FILLING

MINI BAKED POTATOES

3 small baking potatoes

oil and salt, for brushing

CRANBERRY & TURKEY FILLING

1 tsp cranberry sauce

1 tbsp smooth peanut butter

1 tsp milk

2oz (60g) shredded cooked turkey

TUNA & CORN FILLING

⅓ cup (60g) cooked corn

2 tbsp mayonnaise

2oz (60g) flaked tuna, drained

1 scallion, finely sliced

freshly ground black pepper

1 tbsp grated Cheddar cheese

BARBECUE BEAN FILLING

8oz (250g) canned barbecue baked beans, or plain baked beans seasoned with Worcestershire sauce

1 tbsp grated Cheddar cheese

Small baked potatoes look especially attractive when made into little sailboats decorated with a cheese triangle sail and a red pepper flag. Each of the fillings suggested here is enough for 3 potatoes.

1 Wash the potatoes, pat dry, prick with a fork, brush with oil, and sprinkle with a little salt. Place in the preheated oven and bake for about 40 minutes, or until crispy on the outside and tender inside (test with a skewer).

2 Cut the potatoes in half, scoop out the flesh into a bowl, and mash thoroughly. Mix the ingredients from your chosen topping with the mashed potato, then spoon the mixture back into the skins. If using grated cheese, sprinkle a little over each of the potatoes.

3 Place the potatoes under a preheated broiler (they can be arranged in a muffin tin to keep them upright). Heat for a few minutes, or just until they are lightly golden on top. If desired, decorate the potatoes as boats, securing the cheese sails with toothpicks.

 Preparation/cooking
10 minutes/45 minutes

 Oven temperature
400°F/200°C

 Makes 6 portions

 Nutritional information
Rich source of folic acid, protein, and vitamin B12.
(For Cranberry & Turkey Filling)
Rich source of folic acid, protein, and vitamin B12.
(For Tuna & Corn Filling)
Rich source of folic acid, fiber, and protein.
(For Barbecue Bean Filling)

 Suitable for freezing
undecorated only

— NOTE —
If decorating as sailboats, remove the toothpicks as soon as you serve your child's portion.

THOUSAND ISLAND DRESSING

6 tbsp plain yogurt

3 tbsp mayonnaise

3 tbsp ketchup

½ tsp Worcestershire sauce

salt and pepper, to taste

This versatile dressing goes well with a green salad or sliced tomatoes and avocado. You could add 1 tablespoon of finely chopped parsley to garnish.

Blend all the ingredients together, transfer to a clean container, and refrigerate, or whisk thoroughly and use immediately.

 Preparation
2 minutes

 Makes 4 portions

 Nutritional information
Rich source of vitamin B12 and vitamin E.

ANNABEL'S PASTA SALAD

5oz (150g) pasta bows (farfalle)

2oz (60g) green beans

½ cup (60g) sliced carrots

½ cup (100g) frozen corn

4 cherry tomatoes, quartered

DRESSING

2 tbsp (30g) grated onion

4 tbsp vegetable oil

1 tbsp white wine vinegar

2 tbsp water

½ tsp chopped fresh ginger

1 tbsp chopped celery

1 tbsp soy sauce

1½ tsp tomato paste

1 tsp superfine sugar

salt and pepper, to taste

This salad's delicious dressing is popular with my children as a dip for raw vegetables (I make a bottle of it to keep in the refrigerator). The salad is great for lunch boxes, picnics, or as a side dish served warm or cold. Use three-color pasta, if possible.

1 Bring a pot of lightly salted water to a boil, add the pasta, and cook until tender, about 10 minutes, or according to package instructions.

2 Meanwhile, put the beans and carrots in a steamer and cook for 4 minutes. Add the corn to the steamer and cook for 3–4 minutes, or until tender.

3 Combine all the ingredients for the dressing in a blender or food processor, adding only a little salt and pepper, and process until smooth. Combine the cooked pasta with the vegetables and cherry tomatoes and toss with some of the dressing.

VARIATION

Add 2 tbsp (30g) diced cucumber, ½ cup (75g) diced cold chicken or tuna to this salad, and vary the vegetables, according to taste.

  Preparation/cooking
10 minutes/12 minutes

 Makes 4 portions

 Nutritional information
Rich source of beta-carotene, fiber, and folic acid.

See page 104 for main illustration.

PENNE WITH CORN, TUNA & TOMATO

7oz (200g) canned tuna in oil

1 garlic clove, crushed

1 small onion, sliced

6oz (175g) pasta quills (penne)

1½ cups (400g) canned chopped tomatoes

1 tbsp tomato paste

2 tbsp chopped fresh parsley

¾ cup (125g) frozen corn

salt and pepper, to taste

¼ cup (30g) freshly grated Parmesan

This is a simple, popular pasta dish that can be rustled up using mainly ingredients in the pantry. I like to make this using light meat (yellow) tuna.

1 Drain the oil from the tuna into a skillet and set it over low heat. Add the garlic and onion and sauté until softened.

2 Meanwhile, bring a pot of lightly salted water to a boil, add the pasta, and cook until tender, about 9 minutes, or according to package instructions.

3 Add the tomatoes, tomato paste, and parsley to the skillet, and cook for 10 minutes. Add the corn and let the sauce simmer for 5 minutes. Flake the tuna into a bowl, then mix with the sauce and season lightly.

4 Drain the pasta and toss it with the sauce. Spoon into an ovenproof dish, sprinkle with Parmesan, and set under a preheated broiler for 2–3 minutes, until bubbling and golden.

 Preparation/cooking
5 minutes/25 minutes

 Makes 4 portions

Nutritional information
Rich source of calcium, fiber, iron, protein, B vitamins, incl. B12, and zinc.

Pasta with Zucchini, Peppers & Sausages

1 tbsp vegetable oil

1 small onion, sliced

½ small red pepper, cut into diamond shapes

1 small zucchini, sliced

1¼ cups (300ml) tomato passata

½ chicken bouillon cube, finely crumbled

4oz (125g) pasta bows (farfalle)

3½oz (100g) sausages, cooked and sliced

1 Heat the oil in a skillet, add the onion, and sauté until softened. Add the pepper and cook for 3–4 minutes. Add the zucchini and cook for 3 minutes more.

2 Pour the passata into the skillet, then stir in the crumbled bouillon cube. Bring the mixture to a boil, then cover and simmer for 10 minutes.

3 Meanwhile, bring a pot of lightly salted water to a boil, add the pasta, and cook until tender, about 10 minutes, or according to package instructions.

4 Add the sliced sausages to the sauce and cook just until heated through. Drain the pasta, toss it with the sauce, and serve.

  Preparation/cooking
10 minutes/18 minutes

 Makes 4 portions

Nutritional information
Rich source of beta-carotene, fiber, folic acid, protein, and vitamin B12.

Vegetable Lasagna

1 tbsp olive oil

1 onion, chopped

2 garlic cloves, crushed

1 cup (150g) chopped zucchini

1 small eggplant, chopped

2 cups (150g) sliced mushrooms

1 red pepper, chopped

1½ cups (400g) canned chopped tomatoes

2 tsp mixed dried herbs

1 tbsp tomato paste

⅓ cup (90ml) water

salt and pepper, to taste

1¼ cups (125g) broccoli florets

2 batches cheese sauce (see page 71)

12 sheets oven-ready lasagna

¼ cup (30g) grated cheese

The whole family will enjoy this vegetarian lasagna. I make it in a fairly deep dish to create plenty of layers.

1 Heat the oil in a skillet, add the onion and garlic, and sauté for about 1 minute. Add all the vegetables up to and including the red pepper and sauté, stirring occasionally, for about 5 minutes.

2 Add the chopped tomatoes, mixed herbs, tomato paste, and water. Season and then simmer for about 15 minutes. Add the broccoli and cook for 15 minutes, or until all the vegetables are tender. Meanwhile, warm the cheese sauce.

3 To assemble, spoon a third of the vegetables over the bottom of a 9 x 6 x 3in (23 x 15 x 7cm) ovenproof dish. Cover with 4 overlapping sheets of lasagna, then add a third of the cheese sauce. Repeat the layering twice, finishing with a layer of cheese sauce.

4 Sprinkle the grated cheese on top of the final layer of cheese sauce. Transfer to the preheated oven and bake for 40 minutes.

 Preparation/cooking
25 minutes/1 hour 15 minutes

 Oven temperature
350°F/180°C

 Makes 8 portions

 Nutritional information
Rich source of beta-carotene, calcium, fiber, protein, B vitamins, incl. B12, and zinc.

 Suitable for freezing

GOLDEN TURKEY FINGERS

½lb (250g) turkey cutlets

juice of 1 lime or ½ lemon

1 shallot, sliced

flour, to coat

salt and pepper, to taste

¾ cup (75g) dry bread crumbs

1½ tbsp snipped fresh chives

1 egg, lightly beaten

vegetable oil for shallow frying

1 Cut the turkey into ⅜in (1cm) strips. Place in a bowl with the lime or lemon juice and shallot. Cover and refrigerate for 30 minutes.

2 Spread some flour on a plate and season with salt and pepper. On another plate, mix together the bread crumbs and chives. Dip the turkey strips first in the seasoned flour, then in the beaten egg, and then in the bread crumb and chive mixture.

3 Heat the oil in a skillet, add the turkey strips, and sauté until golden and cooked through, about 10 minutes.

  Preparation/cooking
40 minutes/10 minutes

 Makes 4 portions

 Nutritional information
Rich source of folic acid, protein, B vitamins, incl. B6 and B12, and zinc.

Suitable for freezing
uncooked

HEART-SHAPED CHICKEN NUGGETS

¾lb (375g) chicken cutlets, cut into chunks

1 large onion, diced

2 tbsp chopped fresh parsley

1 small apple, peeled and grated

¾ cup (45g) fresh white bread crumbs

1 chicken bouillon cube, crumbled

½ cup 60g) dry bread crumbs

2oz (60g) cheese and onion flavored chips, finely crushed

vegetable oil for frying

The addition of apple gives these nuggets a delicious, moist flavor. If you don't have a heart-shaped cutter, try another shape, but keep to fairly simple lines.

1 Put the first 6 ingredients in a food processor and chop for a few seconds until well combined. Shape the mixture into a flat disk.

2 Use a 2⅜in (6cm) cookie cutter to press out heart shapes. Mix the bread crumbs and chips on a plate, and press the pieces into the coating.

3 Heat enough oil in a large skillet for shallow frying. Add the nuggets and cook for about 6 minutes, turning occasionally, until lightly golden and cooked through.

  Preparation/cooking
25 minutes/6 minutes

 Makes 8 portions

 Nutritional information
Rich source of protein and B vitamins.

Suitable for freezing

CARAMELIZED CHICKEN BREASTS

1 tbsp vegetable oil

1 onion, sliced

1 garlic clove, crushed

salt and pepper, to taste

2 chicken cutlets

1½ tbsp malt vinegar

1½ tbsp ketchup

1½ tbsp soy sauce

2 tbsp water

1½ tbsp honey

1 Heat the oil in an ovenproof pan, add the onion and garlic, and sauté until soft. Season the chicken, add to the pan, and sauté until sealed and golden. Cover, transfer to the preheated oven, and cook for 20 minutes, or until tender.

2 Set the chicken aside and place the pan over high heat. Add the vinegar, bring to a boil, and cook for 1 minute, or until reduced by half.

3 Stir in the ketchup, soy sauce, and water and simmer for 2 minutes. Stir in the honey and cook for 2 minutes. Return the chicken to the sauce to heat it through.

  Preparation/cooking
5 minutes/30 minutes

 Oven temperature
350°F/180°C

 Makes 4 portions

 Nutritional information
Rich source of folic acid, protein, B vitamins, and zinc.

Suitable for freezing

TERIYAKI CHICKEN STIR-FRY

10oz (300g) chicken cutlets

1½ tbsp vegetable oil

1 small onion, sliced

1 garlic clove, crushed

2oz (60g) baby corn

1 small carrot, cut into strips

2oz (60g) cauliflower florets

1 small zucchini, cut into strips

3 tbsp strong chicken stock

MARINADE

1 tbsp soy sauce

1 tbsp oyster sauce

½ tsp brown sugar

1 tsp sesame oil

1 scallion, finely chopped

¼ tsp chopped fresh ginger

1 Cut the chicken breasts into thin strips. Combine the marinade ingredients in a dish with the chicken and leave for at least 30 minutes.

2 Heat the vegetable oil in a lidded wok or large skillet, add the onion and garlic, and stir-fry, uncovered, for 2 minutes.

3 Add the chicken to the wok with the marinade and stir-fry just until the chicken changes color. Quarter the baby corn and add to the wok with the carrots and cauliflower, stir-fry for 3 minutes, then add the zucchini and continue to cook for 2 minutes.

4 Pour in the chicken stock. Cover the wok and cook for 2 minutes, or until the vegetables are tender and the chicken is cooked through.

VARIATION

Replace the chicken with ¾lb (375g) beef fillet, pounded until tender and cut into strips.

 Preparation/cooking
40 minutes, incl. 30 minutes marinating/ 15 minutes

 Makes 4 portions

Nutritional information
Rich source of folic acid, iron, protein, vitamin A, B vitamins, vitamin C, and zinc.

CHICKEN CATERPILLAR KABOBS

4 chicken cutlets, cubed

14oz (425g) canned litchis

1 red pepper, seeded and cut into triangles

MARINADE

3 tbsp soy sauce

3 tbsp honey

½ tbsp lemon juice

TO DECORATE

8 scallion fans (see right)

8 cherry tomatoes or radishes

16 whole cloves

1 Mix the marinade ingredients together in a shallow dish. Add the chicken and marinate for at least 30 minutes. Soak 8 bamboo skewers in water while the chicken marinates.

2 Thread the chicken onto the skewers, putting half a litchi and a red pepper triangle between each piece of chicken. Arrange on a baking sheet and transfer to the preheated oven. Cook for about 15 minutes, basting with the marinade and turning them occasionally, until cooked through.

3 To decorate, make a face for each caterpillar using a tomato or radish, studded with clove eyes. Attach it to the tip of the skewer and thread on a scallion tail. Remove the cloves before your child eats.

 Preparation/cooking
40 minutes, incl. 30 minutes marinating/ 15 minutes

 Oven temperature
350°F/180°C

 Makes 8 portions

Nutritional information
Rich source of beta-carotene, iron, protein, B vitamins, vitamin C, and zinc.

TIP
To make scallion fans, cut them into 3in (7cm) lengths. Make 4 slashes at one end. Place in ice water until the ends curl.

ANNABEL'S TASTY MEATBALLS

1lb (500g) lean ground beef

1 onion, finely chopped

1 tbsp chopped fresh parsley

1 chicken bouillon cube dissolved in 2 tbsp hot water

1 small apple, peeled and grated

½ tsp Worcestershire sauce

pinch of brown sugar

salt and pepper, to taste

flour for coating

vegetable oil for frying

These meatballs are easy to prepare and delicious (the apple keeps them wonderfully moist). They are good on their own or served with spaghetti and Special Tomato Sauce (see page 122).

1 In a mixing bowl, combine all the ingredients except for the flour and vegetable oil. Use your hands to form the mixture into about 24 walnut-size balls. Spread the flour on a plate and coat the meatballs.

2 Heat the oil in a skillet, add the meatballs, and cook over high heat for about 3 minutes, until browned on all sides. Lower the heat a little and cook for 12 minutes, or until cooked through.

 Preparation/cooking
10 minutes/15 minutes

 Makes 8 portions

 Nutritional information
Rich source of folic acid, iron, protein, B vitamins, incl. B12, and zinc.

 Suitable for freezing

HUNGARIAN GOULASH

flour for coating

salt and pepper, to taste

1lb (500g) lean beef, cut into cubes

2 tbsp vegetable oil

2 onions, peeled and chopped

1 red pepper, seeded and chopped

¼lb (250g) mushrooms, sliced

1 tbsp paprika

1¼ cups (400ml) chicken stock (see page 46) or beef stock

3 tbsp tomato paste

1 tbsp ketchup

1 tsp Worcestershire sauce

2 tbsp chopped fresh parsley

6 tbsp sour cream

7oz (200g) pasta, such as tagliatelle

For young children, chop the meat and vegetables into small pieces or process in a blender for just a few seconds. Serve with pasta or noodles.

1 Spread the flour on a plate, season lightly, and use to coat the beef. Heat the vegetable oil in a flameproof casserole, add the beef, and sauté until browned all over. Remove the meat with a slotted spoon and set aside.

2 Add the onions to the casserole and sauté for 5 minutes. Add the red pepper and sauté for 3–4 minutes, then add the mushrooms and cook for 3 more minutes. Sprinkle the paprika over the mixture and cook for about 2 minutes.

3 Return the meat to the casserole, pour in the stock, and stir in the tomato paste, ketchup, Worcestershire sauce, and chopped parsley. Cover, transfer to the preheated oven and cook for about 2 hours. Check that the meat is tender. Season to taste and stir in the sour cream. Set aside and keep warm.

4 Bring a large pot of lightly salted water to a boil, add the pasta, and cook until tender, about 8 minutes, or according to package instructions. Drain, arrange a bed of pasta on each plate, and top with a serving of goulash.

 Preparation/cooking
15 minutes/2 hours 20 minutes

 Oven temperature
300°F/150°C

 Makes 8 portions

 Nutritional information
Rich source of beta-carotene, folic acid, iron, protein, B vitamins, incl. B12, and zinc.

 Suitable for freezing

STICKY TOFFEE PUDDING

3 tbsp (45g) butter

⅔ cup (140g) light brown sugar

2 eggs

1½ cups (175g) flour, sifted

¼ tsp baking powder

1 cup (200ml) boiling water

1 cup (140g) pitted dates

¼ tsp baking soda

¼ tsp vanilla extract

BUTTERSCOTCH SAUCE

½ cup (100g) light brown sugar

4 tbsp (65g) butter

½ cup (125ml) heavy cream

This is one of those classic sticky comfort foods that never fails to please children and adults alike.

1 Cream together the butter and sugar. Beat the eggs into the mixture, then fold in the flour and baking powder.

2 Pour the boiling water over the dates and add the baking soda and vanilla extract. Add this mixture to the batter and blend well.

3 Butter a 11 x 7in (28 x 18cm) ovenproof dish. Pour the batter into the dish and bake in the preheated oven for 40 minutes.

4 To make the sauce, put the brown sugar, butter, and cream in a pan and heat gently for about 5 minutes. Remove the pudding from the oven, add half the sauce, and place under a hot broiler until it bubbles. Serve the remaining sauce separately.

 Preparation/cooking
10 minutes/40 minutes

 Oven temperature
375°F/190°C

 Makes 8 portions

 Nutritional information
Rich source of vitamin B12.

 Suitable for freezing

TIP

This can be made in advance, kept in the refrigerator, and reheated before serving.

CHOCOLATE ORANGE MINI MUFFINS

1 cup (125g) self-rising flour

2 tbsp cocoa powder

¼lb (125g) soft margarine or butter

½ cup (100g) superfine sugar

2 eggs, lightly beaten

grated zest of 1 small orange

½ cup (60g) semisweet chocolate chips

Mini muffins are just the right size for small children. However, if you prefer, you can also bake these in medium muffin tins. They will make about 15 muffins.

1 Sift the flour and cocoa together. Cream the margarine and sugar. Add the eggs to the creamed mixture, a little at a time, together with a tablespoon of the flour mixture.

2 Mix in the remaining flour and cocoa until blended. Stir in the orange zest and chocolate chips. Line some muffin tins with fluted paper cups and fill each of the cups two thirds full. Transfer to the preheated oven and cook for 10–12 minutes.

 Preparation/cooking
20 minutes/12 minutes

 Oven temperature
350°F/180°C

 Makes 30 mini muffins
or 15 medium muffins

 Nutritional information
Rich source of vitamin B12.

 Suitable for freezing

PIGGY CAKE
Use pink-tinted ready-made fondant icing and halved marshmallows to make this animal face, as described below.

PORCUPINE CAKE
Make a spiky porcupine with chocolate buttercream icing set with broken flaked chocolate sticks.

CLOWN FACE
Decorate a white-iced cake with yellow grated icing hair, a red icing nose and mouth, and black writing icing eyes.

CHARACTER CAKES

8 tbsp (125g) soft margarine or butter

½ cup (125g) superfine sugar

2 eggs

1 tsp vanilla extract

½ tsp grated lemon zest

1 cup (125g) self-rising flour

⅓ cup (60g) raisins (optional)

TO DECORATE AS PIGS

pink food coloring

6oz (175g) ready-made fondant white icing, plus confectioners' sugar to dust

3 tbsp apricot jam, strained and warmed gently

pink marshmallows

colored writing icing

red licorice laces

Decorated cakes are great for parties. Here I describe how to make a piggy face, but you could try clowns, spiky chocolate porcupines, or ladybugs made with red and black icing. Older children will enjoy helping decorate these.

1 Cream the margarine and sugar until pale and fluffy. Beat in the eggs one at a time, then add the vanilla extract and lemon zest.

2 Fold in the flour and raisins, if using, and mix until soft and creamy.

3 Line a cupcake pan with fluted paper cups and half fill each. Transfer to the preheated oven and bake for about 20 minutes. Let cool on a wire rack.

4 Knead a little of the pink food coloring into the icing until an even color tone is achieved. Lightly dust a work surface with confectioners' sugar and roll out the fondant until it is about ⅛in (2.5mm) thick.

5 Use a glass to cut out disks of icing slightly larger than the cakes. Brush the cake tops with a little warmed apricot jam and put the icing on top.

6 Make a pig's snout by attaching a marshmallow, cut in half, to the center of the cake using jam; draw on nostrils and eyes with writing icing. Add halved marshmallow ears and a short strip of licorice for the mouth.

 Preparation/cooking
20 minutes/20 minutes plus decorating time

 Oven temperature
350°F/180°C

 Makes 15 cakes

 Nutritional information
Rich source of vitamin A and vitamin B12.

 Suitable for freezing
before decorating

TIP
Ready-made fondant icing is easy to tint by kneading in a few drops of food coloring, as described in step 4.

PACKAGE BIRTHDAY CAKE

4 batches sponge cake batter (see Character Cakes, opposite)

FILLING

1 cup (250g) raspberry jam

1 batch buttercream made with 6 tbsp (175g) soft butter beaten with 3 cups (375g) confectioners' sugar, 1 tbsp milk, and 1 tsp vanilla extract

TO DECORATE

red, blue, green, and yellow food coloring

2¼lb (1.25kg) ready-made fondant icing (see left), plus confectioners' sugar to dust

8 tbsp apricot jam, strained and warmed gently

1 Pour the sponge batter into a greased and waxed paper-lined 8in (20cm) square pan and a 9 x 5 x 3in (23 x 12 x 7cm) loaf pan. Put in the preheated oven; bake the loaf for 45 minutes and the square for 1 hour. Remove from the pans and let cool on a rack.

2 Divide the loaf cake into the desired number of blocks to form small packages. Slice all the cakes across and sandwich the halves together with a layer each of raspberry jam and buttercream.

3 Choose your color scheme, then tint the fondant, as described in step 4 of the previous recipe.

4 Brush the top and sides of the cake blocks with apricot jam. Lay the icing over the top, either in a single sheet or in strips for a striped effect. Make icing bows in contrasting colors, sticking them down with jam. Decorate further with icing disks or flowers, or leave plain. Perhaps add a few marzipan animals.

Preparation/cooking
20 minutes/1 hour plus decorating time

Oven temperature
350°F/180°C

Makes 20 portions

Nutritional information
Rich source of vitamin A and vitamin B12.

See page 105 for illustration.

SHORTBREAD COOKIES

1 stick (125g) butter (cold)

¼ cup (60g) superfine sugar

¼ cup (30g) ground almonds

pinch of salt

⅔ cup (90g) flour, plus flour to dust

¼ cup (60g) cornstarch

glacé icing or confectioners' sugar, to decorate (optional)

1 Beat the butter and sugar together until fluffy. Add the remaining ingredients and beat until the mixture sticks together and begins to form a ball.

2 Dust a pastry board with flour, turn out the mixture, and knead gently for 1–2 minutes to form a smooth dough. Roll the dough out until ¼in (5mm) thick. Cut into shapes using cookie cutters.

3 Using a narrow spatula, transfer the shapes to a greased baking sheet. Bake in the preheated oven for 15 minutes, or until lightly golden. Let cool on a wire rack, then lift off. Ice or decorate, as desired.

Preparation/cooking
15 minutes/15 minutes

Oven temperature
350°F/180°C

Makes 12–15 cookies

Nutritional information
Rich source of vitamin A.

Suitable for freezing

See page 121 for further illustration.

3-5
Years

Once your child begins to interact
more with her peers, perhaps when she
starts nursery school, you may find you no
longer have complete control over
what she eats. However, if you continue to
encourage her to eat a varied diet at
home and keep introducing new and
exciting recipes, you will have a
happy, healthy eater.

A menu planner for each age group begins on page 132

The Preschool Child

THE GREATEST CHANGE in your child's life at this stage of development will probably be starting nursery school, and at this point, eating has to fit into more of a routine. Nursery-age children will need a good breakfast to keep them alert until lunchtime. Packed lunches may soon become an essential part of your child's diet too, and they will need to be nutritious and sustaining. This is an exciting age: your child will be learning new skills, and it is the perfect time to consolidate good eating habits, encourage diversity, and involve children in cooking.

A healthy and varied diet

Between the ages of 3 and 5 your child's manual dexterity should greatly improve and she should be able to master all the basic eating skills. She should also have her first full set of teeth. Around this age many children will start noticing commercials that push unhealthy foods. This is a good time to explain the basic principles of nutrition to your child.

If parents offer fresh fruits and vegetables in a defensive or apologetic way, children will begin to reject them. So if you can make these fresh foods seem to be the appealing, tasty foods they really are, then your child will not equate "healthy" with "nasty." Vitamins are no substitute for fresh fruits and vegetables in your child's diet.

AVOIDING PROBLEMS

Children are great mimics and will be affected by adult attitudes to eating. If parents do not eat healthy food themselves, or refuse to try new dishes, children are likely to copy their conservative eating habits. If a member of the family is dieting, don't discuss it in front of the children. You need to avoid creating eating anxieties.

The good breakfast guide

Nutritionists generally agree that an adequate breakfast is necessary for proper physical and mental functioning. Many children have their last meal around 5 P.M. and may not eat until 7 A.M. the next day. They will have fasted for

14 hours, and their brain will need a jump start to prepare for the demands of the day ahead. A whole grain cereal is best, such as wheat flakes (see page 12). Alternatively, offer whole grain toast with an egg or cheese.

FRUIT & JUICE

Offer a variety of fresh and dried fruits, and add them to milkshakes and cereals. Try serving fruit in new ways: put half a kiwi in an egg cup so your child can scoop out the flesh with a spoon.

OATMEAL
WITH JAM

BOILED EGG
AND TOAST

CEREAL
WITH MILK

MUESLI, FRUIT,
AND YOGURT

ORANGE
JUICE

Outside the home

Some time after her third birthday, if not well before, your child may be looked after by a caregiver or go to nursery school. If lunch is provided, check that it is well-balanced and nutritious. If a picnic lunch is required, try to make it interesting and healthy. Young children like miniature portions, so individual cheeses, tiny boxes of raisins, or mini muffins are useful additions.

PICNIC FOOD
Portions should be easy to eat and not too messy.

A chicken drumstick is ideal for lunch

PACKING PORTABLE FOODS

Warm conditions encourage the growth of bacteria, so it's essential to keep picnic lunches cool, especially if you have included cooked meats. An insulated bag with an ice pack would be ideal, or a small carton of frozen juice can be packed with sandwiches to keep them cool. By the time your child is ready to eat lunch, the juice should have defrosted.

BRIEFING CAREGIVERS

If you find that your child is always overhungry when she gets out of preschool, ask a teacher or sitter to monitor what she eats and report back to you. Children are usually quite hungry after a preschool day and it can be a good time to encourage them to snack healthily. You can bring a nutritious snack, such as a banana or a cheese and tomato sandwich, when you pick up your child, and you will usually find that she will eat it eagerly. If you have a policy of no candy or chocolate between meals, then let sitters and relatives know so that you can be consistent with your rules. You might suggest other treats, such as exotic fruits or homemade cookies.

It may not be a good idea to ban sweets altogether, because there is a danger of making them into an even more desirable "forbidden fruit." It is probably easier to limit sweets to certain times, such as after meals and on weekends.

FAST FOOD

Children are eating more "fast food" than ever before. Many of these foods are high in calories, salt, or sugar, but low in nutrients. To encourage young fast food addicts to eat a nutritious diet, make healthy versions of their fast food favorites, such as Mini Pizzas (see page 91), Crunchy Chicken Fingers (see page 96), Oven-Baked Fries (see page 125), and Ice Pops (see page 99).

REMEMBER

◆ SEE THAT YOUR CHILD eats a substantial breakfast, particularly on weekdays if she will be at nursery school. If she is a very slow eater and you are short of time, give her a sandwich or a healthy muffin that she can eat on the way.

◆ INSURE THAT FOOD in your child's lunch is kept cool and well-wrapped so that it stays free from bacteria.

◆ WHEN SETTING UP a healthy eating plan, enlist the help of visitors, grandparents, and other caregivers. If everyone is aware of your food policies, your child will be treated consistently.

International Tastes

TRY TO INTRODUCE EXCITING FLAVORS and new dishes periodically so that your child's tastes and horizons are continually broadened and enriched. Many children are eager to experience new foods at this age, and there are wonderful dishes from all around the world that make easy family meals. It may even give you the opportunity to talk with your child about different countries and their cultures.

An all-in-one tasty rice dish

SLEEPING CANNELLONI

Introduce this Italian classic with a few decorative touches that will add instant child appeal. The stuffed cannelloni tubes have the usual "blanket" of cheese, but little mushroom faces and black olive boots carry the theme to a humorous point.
(See page 122 for recipe.)

Use freshly grated cheese to make the hair and decorate with pepper bows

A band of tomato sauce makes a quick turned down "sheet"

VEGETABLE SAMOSAS

These crispy Indian-style packages hide a filling of mildly spiced chopped vegetables. They are good as a hot or cold snack.
(See page 124 for recipe.)

Crunchy corn taco shells are an excellent pantry staple for children

BEEF TACOS
Crispy corn tacos stuffed with ground beef or chicken strips, beans, and salad are popular with children. The filling in these tacos has a hint of chili and cilantro to give it a little kick. (See page 129 for recipe.)

An irresistible combination of ingredients that is fun to eat

PAELLA
Give dinner a Spanish flavor with this festive one-pot meal of chicken, sausages, shrimp, and bright yellow rice. (See page 126 for recipe.)

Crisp phyllo pastry

SINGAPORE NOODLES
Curly Chinese noodles, chicken, and shrimp stir-fried with soy sauce and sesame oil combine to create a fast dinner dish that is bursting with flavors. (See page 128 for recipe.)

SLEEPING CANNELLONI

½lb (250g) frozen spinach

2 tbsp (30g) butter

1 onion, finely chopped

1 small garlic clove, crushed

2 cups (125g) sliced mushrooms

1 tbsp flour

⅓ cup (90ml) milk

2 tbsp light cream

salt and pepper, to taste

8 cannelloni tubes

CHEESE SAUCE

2 tbsp (30g) butter

¼ cup (30g) flour

2 cups (450ml) milk

½ cup (60g) each grated Gruyère and Cheddar cheese

½ tsp dry mustard

salt and pepper, to taste

TO DECORATE

ready-made tomato sauce (e.g., passata), 8 sautéed mushrooms, handful of grated Cheddar, 8 black olives, tiny green pepper bows and squares, and red pepper strips

1 Place the spinach in a pot without water, cover, and cook over low heat for 5 minutes, or according to package instructions. Squeeze out any excess water.

2 Melt the butter in a skillet, add the onion and garlic, and sauté until softened. Add the mushrooms and cook for 5 minutes. Stir in the flour and cook for 1 minute. Add the cooked spinach, stir in the milk, and cook for 2 minutes. Remove the skillet from the heat, stir in the cream, and season to taste.

3 Lightly grease a 10 x 8in (25 x 20cm) ovenproof dish. Use a teaspoon to fill the cannelloni tubes with the stuffing, then arrange them in the dish in a single layer.

4 To make the sauce, melt the butter in a pan over low heat, add the flour, and stir to make a paste. Cook gently for 2 minutes, then whisk in the milk and cook, stirring, until thickened. Remove from the heat, stir in the cheeses until melted, add the mustard, and season to taste.

5 Pour the sauce over the cannelloni, transfer to the preheated oven, and bake for 30 minutes.

6 To decorate, use the tomato sauce to make a turned-down sheet and arrange the olives as feet. Make slits in the mushrooms, push in green pepper eyes and red pepper mouths, and use the grated cheese as hair, adding the green pepper bows.

 Preparation/cooking
35 minutes/45 minutes

 Oven temperature
350°F/180°C

 Makes 8 portions

 Nutritional information
Rich source of beta-carotene, calcium, folic acid, iron, protein, B vitamins, incl. B12, and zinc.

Suitable for freezing
undecorated

See page 120 for main illustration.

SPECIAL TOMATO SAUCE

1 tsp olive oil

1 garlic clove, chopped

1½ cups (400g) canned tomatoes

2 tbsp pesto

¼ tsp mild chili powder

1 tsp balsamic vinegar

1 tsp superfine sugar

salt and pepper, to taste

1 tbsp shredded fresh basil

2 tbsp freshly grated Parmesan

This full-flavored tomato sauce is wonderfully versatile: try it as a base for pizza, or add a few mini meatballs (see page 112) or a small can of tuna to make a simple pasta sauce.

1 Heat the oil in a skillet over low heat, add the garlic, and sauté for 30 seconds. Stir in the tomatoes and break them up with a spoon. Add the remaining ingredients except the basil and Parmesan. Season, then simmer for 10 minutes.

2 Stir in the basil and Parmesan and cook just until the cheese has melted.

 Preparation/cooking
5 minutes/12 minutes

 Makes 4 portions

 Nutritional information
Rich source of beta-carotene, calcium, protein, and B vitamins.

 Suitable for freezing

PASTA TWISTS WITH ZUCCHINI

1 tbsp olive oil

1 small onion, sliced

1 garlic clove, chopped

1 cup (125g) sliced zucchini

¾ cup (100g) sliced mushrooms

1¼ cups (300ml) tomato passata

½ tsp balsamic vinegar

½ tsp sugar

salt and pepper, to taste

7oz (200g) pasta twists (fusilli)

¼ cup (30g) freshly grated Parmesan

Another quick recipe that will encourage children to enjoy eating vegetables. Vary the vegetables according to seasonal availability.

1 Heat the oil in a skillet, add the onion, garlic, zucchini, and mushrooms, and cook for 7–8 minutes. Stir in the passata, vinegar, and sugar, and season to taste. Simmer, covered, for 15 minutes.

2 Meanwhile, bring a pot of lightly salted water to a boil, add the pasta and cook until tender, about 10 minutes, or according to package instructions.

3 Remove the sauce from the heat, stir in the Parmesan, then toss with the drained pasta.

  Preparation/cooking
10 minutes/25 minutes

 Makes 4 portions

Nutritional information
Rich source of calcium, fiber, and protein.

Suitable for freezing

ITALIAN RISOTTO WITH MUSHROOMS & PEAS

2 tbsp vegetable oil

1 onion, chopped

1 garlic clove, crushed

½ cup (60g) chopped red pepper

1½ cups (100g) sliced mushrooms

1 cup (200g) short-grain rice (Arborio)

3¾ cups (900ml) hot vegetable stock or chicken stock (see page 46)

1 cup (100g) frozen peas

¼ cup (30g) freshly grated Parmesan

1 tbsp (15g) butter

salt and pepper, to taste

To make a good risotto, you need a heavy-bottomed pan that will allow even, slow cooking: a large, fairly deep frying pan is ideal.

1 Heat the oil in a pan over medium-low heat. Add the onion and garlic and cook for 1 minute. Add the pepper and mushrooms and cook for 5 minutes.

2 Add the rice and cook, stirring constantly, for 1 minute, until all the grains are well coated with oil. Pour in a ladleful of hot stock and simmer, stirring constantly, until absorbed.

3 Continue to add small quantities of hot stock, waiting for each ladleful to be absorbed before adding more. Stir frequently to prevent sticking.

4 When all the stock has been added and the rice is almost cooked, about 20–25 minutes, stir in the peas and cook for 3–4 minutes. Stir in the Parmesan and butter, season to taste, and serve.

VARIATION

Omit the peas and add ¼lb (125g) cooked, finely sliced ham just before adding the Parmesan.

   Preparation/cooking
10 minutes/40 minutes

Makes 4 portions

Nutritional information
Rich source of beta-carotene, calcium, folic acid, and protein.

TIP
If you want to prepare the risotto in advance, only add half the stock and remove from the heat. Add the remaining stock gradually and continue to cook just before you want to serve the risotto.

MILDLY SPICED VEGETABLE SAMOSAS

½ tbsp vegetable oil

½ onion, very finely chopped

½ garlic clove, crushed

¼ tsp each curry powder, ground ginger, and ground cumin

1 cup (75g) finely chopped mushrooms

¾ cup (90g) cauliflower, cut into very small florets

1 carrot, very finely chopped

2 tsp superfine sugar

3 tsp plain yogurt

salt and pepper, to taste

12 phyllo pastry sheets

4 tbsp (60g) butter, melted

1 Heat the oil in a skillet, add the onion and garlic, and sauté for 2–3 minutes. Stir in the spices and sauté for 1 minute. Add the vegetables and cook for 5 minutes, stirring occasionally. Stir in the sugar and yogurt. Season and cook for 3–4 minutes.

2 Lay the phyllo pastry out flat and cover with a damp dish towel. Place one sheet of pastry on the work surface and brush with melted butter. Fold the pastry in half lengthwise and brush again with butter.

3 Place a tablespoon of filling on one end of the strip, leaving a 1in (2.5cm) wide border around it. Fold over the corner to make a triangle, then keep folding the package over on itself, along the length of the pastry. Seal the flap left at the end with melted butter. Repeat with the remaining sheets and filling.

4 Place the samosas on a lightly greased baking sheet and brush with more butter. Bake in the preheated oven for 20–25 minutes, or until crisp.

 Preparation/cooking
35 minutes/35 minutes

 Oven temperature
350°F/180°C

 Makes 8 portions

 Nutritional information
Rich source of beta-carotene.

 Suitable for freezing
uncooked

—— TIP ——
When handling phyllo pastry, keep the piece you are not working with covered with a damp dish towel to prevent it from drying out and becoming brittle and difficult to work with.

MINI BEAN & VEGGIE ENCHILADAS

1 tbsp vegetable oil

½ onion, chopped

1 small garlic clove, crushed

¼ red chili, finely chopped (optional)

7oz (200g) canned red kidney beans or refried beans

½ cup (125g) cooked corn

¼ cup (200g) canned chopped tomatoes, drained

salt and pepper, to taste

1 tbsp chopped fresh parsley

4 mini flour tortillas

3 tbsp (45g) grated Cheddar cheese

Small flour tortillas can be bought and then filled with a variety of ingredients. Kidney beans are a good protein source, and are rich in iron.

1 Heat the oil in a skillet, add the onion, garlic, and chili, if using, and cook gently for 3 minutes.

2 Roughly chop the kidney beans. Add the beans to the skillet with the corn and chopped tomatoes. Season to taste and cook over medium heat for 5 minutes. Sprinkle with parsley.

3 Divide the filling among the tortillas, roll them up, and top with cheese. Heat through in a microwave for 1–2 minutes, or in a conventional oven for 6 minutes, then broil until golden and bubbly.

VARIATION

Replace the beans with 2 chicken cutlets, cut into strips, seasoned, and fried. Replace the corn and tomatoes with half a small red pepper, chopped and sautéed. Heat the enchiladas through, then dress with a spoonful each of salsa and sour cream.

 Preparation/cooking
10 minutes/15 minutes

 Oven temperature
microwave on high or conventional oven at 350°F/180°C

 Makes 4 portions

 Nutritional information
Rich source of beta-carotene, calcium, fiber, folic acid, iron, protein, vitamin C, and zinc.

FISH & OVEN-BAKED FRIES

¾lb (350g) small–medium potatoes, scrubbed

3½ tbsp olive oil

freshly ground sea salt and pepper, to taste

flour, to coat

½lb (250g) flounder or cod fillets, cut into chunks

1 lightly beaten egg

1oz (30g) bag salted potato chips, crushed

If you are making these for a special children's party, why not serve them in a cone made from rolled-up paper?

1 Halve the potatoes lengthwise, then cut each piece into 4 sticks. Pour 1½ tablespoons of oil into a roasting pan and place in the preheated oven for 2–3 minutes.

2 Transfer the potatoes to the roasting pan. Toss in the oil until well coated and sprinkle with sea salt. Return to the oven and bake for 30 minutes, or until crisp on the outside but tender.

3 Meanwhile, season the flour and use to coat the fish pieces, then dip them in egg, and roll in the chips. Heat the remaining oil in a skillet, add the fish, and cook thoroughly. Serve with the fries.

 Preparation/cooking
5 minutes/35 minutes

 Oven temperature
400°F/200°C

 Makes 4 portions

 Nutritional information
Rich source of folic acid, protein, vitamin B12, and vitamin E.

TIP
The fish can be fried in advance and then reheated in the oven. It can also be baked on a greased baking sheet for 10–12 minutes.

125

STICKY BAR-B-Q DRUMSTICKS

4 large chicken drumsticks, scored with a knife (remove the skin first if preferred)

MARINADE

½ tbsp vegetable oil

1 small onion, chopped

½ cup (75g) dark brown sugar

juice of ½ lemon

½ tbsp Worcestershire sauce

4 tbsp ketchup

1 tbsp white wine vinegar

Barbecued drumsticks are excellent eaten hot or cold in lunch boxes. Wrap the drumstick ends in foil so that they can be eaten with the fingers.

1 To make the marinade, heat the oil in a skillet, add the onion, and sauté until soft. Stir in the sugar and cook gently for 1–2 minutes. Add the remaining ingredients and simmer for 5 minutes.

2 Pour the mixture into a glass or ceramic bowl, add the drumsticks, and marinate for at least 30 minutes and up to 12 hours.

3 Transfer the drumsticks to a baking dish, baste well, and place under a preheated broiler. Cook for 20 minutes, turning halfway through and basting with the barbecue sauce. Check that they are cooked through, wrap the ends in foil, and serve hot or cold.

 Preparation/cooking
45 minutes, incl.
30 minutes marinating/
20 minutes

 Makes 4 portions

 Nutritional information
Rich source of protein and B vitamins.

 Suitable for freezing

PAELLA

1 tbsp sunflower oil

1 onion, chopped

2 boneless chicken cutlets, cut into chunks

1 red pepper, seeded and chopped

1½ cups (300g) long-grain rice

1 tsp turmeric

1 tsp mild chili powder

2 celery stalks, chopped

4½ cups (1 liter) chicken stock (see page 46)

1 bay leaf

1 cup (100g) frozen peas

2 pork sausages, broiled

¼lb (125g) small cooked, peeled shrimp

salt and pepper, to taste

This is a great all-in-one dish that's easy to cook and full of flavor. The turmeric gives the rice a rich yellow tint.

1 Heat the oil in a deep, heavy-bottomed skillet, add the onion, and sauté for 1 minute. Add the chicken and sauté until seared on all sides.

2 Add the red pepper and cook, stirring, for 1 minute. Stir in the rice, turmeric, chili powder, and celery and sauté for 1 minute, stirring the mixture constantly.

3 Pour in the stock, add the bay leaf, stir well, then simmer for 15–20 minutes, uncovered, until all the liquid is absorbed.

4 Add the peas to the skillet and cook for 2–3 minutes. Slice the sausages on the diagonal and then add to the rice with the shrimp and seasoning. Allow to heat through, remove the bay leaf, and serve.

 Preparation/cooking
10 minutes/25 minutes

 Makes 8 portions

 Nutritional information
Rich source of beta-carotene, folic acid, protein, vitamin E, and zinc.

 Suitable for freezing

See page 120 for illustration.

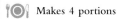 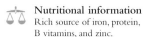

CHICKEN SATAY

2 chicken cutlets, cut
into chunks

MARINADE

2 tbsp Chinese yellow bean
sauce

2 tbsp soy sauce

2 tbsp peanut butter

1 tbsp rice wine vinegar

2 tbsp honey

Thread vegetable chunks, perhaps pieces of onion or pepper, onto the skewers, if desired.

1 Mix all the marinade ingredients with the chicken in a glass or ceramic bowl. Let marinate for at least 30 minutes. Soak 4 bamboo skewers in water while the chicken marinates.

2 Thread the chicken onto the skewers and cook under a preheated broiler for 8–10 minutes, until cooked through, turning and basting occasionally with the marinade.

Preparation/cooking
35 minutes, incl.
30 minutes marinating/
10 minutes

Makes 4 portions

Nutritional information
Rich source of iron, protein,
B vitamins, and zinc.

NOTE
Remove the skewers before
serving to young children.

EGG-FRIED RICE WITH CHICKEN & SHRIMP

1 cup (175g) basmati rice,
rinsed in cold water,
then drained

4 tbsp vegetable oil

1 small onion, finely chopped

½ cup (60g) finely chopped
red pepper

salt and pepper, to taste

1 beaten egg

½ cup (60g) frozen peas

½ cup (60g) frozen corn

1 large scallion, sliced

1 chicken cutlet, cut into
thin strips

¼lb (125g) cooked shrimp
(optional)

1 tbsp light soy sauce

Egg-fried rice with vegetables and chicken is an appealing, simple meal. Your child may want to practice eating with chopsticks; it will be slow going at first, so provide a fork as well.

1 Bring a pot of lightly salted water to a boil, add the rice, and cook until tender, about 10 minutes.

2 Heat half the oil in a large skillet or wok, add the onion, and sauté for 2 minutes. Add the red pepper and cook for 7–8 minutes. Season the beaten egg with a little pepper, pour it into the skillet, tipping the skillet to spread it evenly, and cook until set. Remove from the heat and break the egg up into small pieces with a wooden spoon.

3 Return the pan to the heat, add the peas and corn, and cook until tender. Remove the egg/vegetable mixture from the pan and set aside. Add the remaining oil and sauté the scallion for 1 minute. Add the shredded chicken and sauté for 3–4 minutes, or until cooked, then season.

4 Add the cooked rice and shrimp, if using, and toss the rice over high heat for 2 minutes. Return the egg/vegetable mixture to the pan, add the soy sauce, and toss together until heated through.

Preparation/cooking
10 minutes/30 minutes

Makes 4 portions

Nutritional information
Rich source of beta-carotene,
folic acid, protein, vitamin
B12, vitamin C, and zinc.

 Suitable for freezing

Your child can begin to learn about different cultures and their traditions, but it may be a while before he masters the art of using chopsticks

SINGAPORE NOODLES

5oz (150g) chicken cutlets

2½ tbsp vegetable oil

1 beaten egg

1 garlic clove, chopped

¼ tsp minced red chili (optional)

2½oz (75g) baby corn

½ cup (75g) each carrots and zucchini, cut into thin strips

¾ cup (125g) bean sprouts

¼ tsp mild curry powder

⅓ cup (90ml) strong chicken stock

3oz (90g) small peeled shrimp

3 scallions, thinly sliced

5oz (150g) Chinese noodles

MARINADE

2 tbsp Teriyaki sauce

½ tsp sugar

1 tsp cornstarch

These noodles can be made spicier with added chili and curry powder. If preferred, replace the shrimp with pork or more chicken. For extra flavor, cook the beaten egg in ½ tablespoon of sesame oil.

1 Mix the marinade ingredients together in a bowl. Cut the chicken into thin strips, add to the bowl, and marinate for at least 30 minutes.

2 Heat ½ tablespoon of oil in a skillet, add the egg, and cook to make a thin omelet. Remove from the pan and cut into ribbons. Heat a tablespoon of oil in the pan or a wok and sauté the garlic and chili, if using, for 30 seconds. Drain the chicken, add to the pan, and cook for 3–4 minutes, then set aside.

3 Heat the remaining oil in the wok. Add the baby corn and carrots and stir-fry for 2 minutes. Add the zucchini and bean sprouts and cook for 2 minutes. Stir the curry powder into the stock and add to the pan. Return the chicken to the pan with the shrimp, scallions, and egg and cook for 2 minutes.

4 Cook the noodles in a pot of boiling water for 3 minutes or according to package instructions. Drain, mix with the stir-fry, and heat through.

 Preparation/cooking
45 minutes, incl. 30 minutes marinating/ 20 minutes

 Makes 4 portions

 Nutritional information
Rich source of beta-carotene, fiber, folic acid, iron, protein, B vitamins, incl. B12, vitamin C, and zinc.

See page 121 for main illustration.

BEEF STIR-FRY WITH OYSTER SAUCE

¾lb (375g) lean beef, cut into strips

1 tbsp corn oil

1 small onion, sliced

1 tbsp sesame oil

1 garlic clove, crushed

1 carrot, cut into strips or stars

¼lb (125g) broccoli florets

¼lb (125g) baby corn

¼lb (125g) snow peas

1 red pepper, cut into strips

MARINADE

1 tbsp oyster sauce

2 tbsp soy sauce

1 tsp light brown sugar

This quick Asian dish uses oyster sauce, but there are other good, commercial stir-fry sauces available – check if they are additive-free.

1 Combine the marinade ingredients in a bowl, then add the beef strips and marinate for 30 minutes. Remove the beef and set aside, reserving the marinade.

2 Meanwhile, heat the corn oil in a wok or skillet. Add half the onion and stir-fry until softened. Add the beef and stir-fry until cooked, then remove and set aside.

3 Heat the sesame oil in the wok and stir-fry the remaining onion and the garlic for 2–3 minutes. Add the carrot, broccoli, and baby corn and stir-fry for 3–4 minutes. Add the snow peas and red pepper, then stir-fry for 3–4 minutes longer.

4 Return the beef strips to the pan, pour on the marinade, and stir-fry for 2–3 minutes more.

 Preparation/cooking
45 minutes, incl. 30 minutes marinating/ 25 minutes

 Makes 4 portions

 Nutritional information
Rich source of beta-carotene, fiber, folic acid, iron, protein, B vitamins, incl. B12, vitamin C, and zinc.

 Suitable for freezing

BEEF TERIYAKI SKEWERS

3 tbsp soy sauce

4 tbsp mirin

1 tsp sesame oil

1 garlic clove, crushed

1in (2.5cm) piece of fresh ginger, grated

10oz (300g) beef fillet, cubed

1 tsp cornstarch

1 Combine all the ingredients except the cornstarch in a bowl and marinate for at least 1 hour. Soak 4 bamboo skewers in water while the steak marinates.

2 Thread the beef onto the skewers, reserving the marinade. Put the skewers on the broiler or barbecue and cook for 4–5 minutes on each side.

3 Meanwhile, mix the cornstarch to a paste with 1 tablespoon of the marinade, then pour into a pan with the remaining marinade. Heat for 2 minutes, or until thickened. Serve as a dipping sauce.

 Preparation/cooking
1 hour 5 minutes, incl.
1 hour marinating/
10 minutes

 Makes 4 portions

 Nutritional information
Rich source of iron, protein, B vitamins, incl. B12, and zinc.

BEEF TACOS

¼lb (125g) lean ground beef

½ small onion, finely diced

½ each red and green pepper, cored, seeded, and finely diced

3½oz (100g) canned red kidney beans

1 tomato, peeled, seeded, and diced

½ tbsp mild chili sauce

½ tbsp chopped fresh cilantro

salt and pepper, to taste

4 taco shells

4 lettuce leaves

1 Heat a dry skillet for 1 minute. Add the ground beef and stir-fry for about 5 minutes, or until cooked through. Add the onion and cook for 2 minutes. Add the red and green peppers and sauté for 2 minutes longer. Stir in the beans, tomato, chili sauce, and half the cilantro. Cook over low heat for 3–4 minutes. Season to taste.

2 Meanwhile, warm the tacos in the preheated oven for 2–3 minutes, or in a microwave on full power for 1 minute. Remove the shells from the oven, line with lettuce, fill with the beef mixture, and garnish with the remaining cilantro.

 Preparation/cooking
10 minutes/15 minutes

 Oven temperature
350°F/180°C

 Makes 4 portions

 Nutritional information
Rich source of beta-carotene, fiber, folic acid, iron, protein, vitamin B12, vitamin C, and zinc.

COUNTRY APPLE CAKE

3 cups (375g) self-rising flour
2 tsp allspice
1½ sticks (175g) butter
1½ cups (300g) cooking apples, peeled, cored, and chopped
1 cup (250g) golden raisins
⅔ cup (150ml) milk
1 cup (175g) light brown sugar
1 egg, lightly beaten
2 tbsp honey
½ tbsp granulated sugar

A crumbly-textured dark apple cake that is perfect for a snack.

1 Sift the flour and allspice into a bowl and rub in the butter using your fingertips.

2 Combine the apples, golden raisins, milk, and brown sugar and stir into the flour mixture. Stir in the beaten egg.

3 Line an 8in (20cm) round cake pan. Spoon the mixture into the pan. Bake in the preheated oven for 1 hour. Remove, leave in the pan for 10 minutes, then transfer to a wire rack to cool.

4 Heat the honey in a small pan and brush it over the top of the cake, then sprinkle with the granulated sugar. Store in an airtight container.

Preparation/cooking
25 minutes/1 hour

Oven temperature
325°F/170°C

Makes 8 portions

Nutritional information
Rich source of calcium, fiber, iron, vitamin A, and vitamin B12.

Suitable for freezing

CHOCOLATE CHIP & ORANGE CUT-OUT COOKIES

1½ sticks (175g) butter (at room temperature)
5 tbsp (75g) confectioners' sugar, sifted
2 cups (225g) self-rising flour, sifted
½ tsp salt
½ tsp grated orange zest
½ cup (60g) semisweet chocolate chips

Children love interestingly shaped cookies and will enjoy helping you cut these out. The subtle orange flavor combines well with the chocolate chips to make these cookies irresistible.

1 Put all the ingredients except the chocolate chips in a food processor and mix until blended together (alternatively, beat together by hand).

2 Mix in the chocolate chips by hand. Knead the dough until pliable, form into a ball, wrap in plastic wrap, and refrigerate for about 1 hour.

3 Roll out the dough to a thickness of ¼in (½cm) and cut into shapes using a variety of cookie cutters. Arrange on a lightly greased baking sheet (or one sprayed with nonstick cooking spray) and bake in the preheated oven for about 10 minutes.

Preparation/cooking
1 hour 15 minutes, incl. 1 hour chilling/ 10 minutes

Oven temperature
350°F/180°C

Makes 25–30 cookies

Nutritional information
Rich source of vitamin A.

Suitable for freezing

CHOCOLATE PROFITEROLES & PUFF PASTRY MICE

PUFF PASTRY

6 tbsp (90g) lightly salted butter, cut into small pieces

1 cup (200ml) water

⅔ cup (90g) all-purpose flour

3 eggs, lightly beaten

CREAM FILLING

2½ cups (600ml) heavy cream

2 tbsp confectioners' sugar

CHOCOLATE ICING

6oz (175g) high-quality semisweet chocolate, broken into small pieces

6 tbsp (90g) unsalted butter, cut into small pieces

TO DECORATE AS MICE (OPTIONAL)

flaked almonds

chocolate chips

glacé cherries

red licorice laces

1 To make the pastry, put the butter and water in a saucepan and slowly bring to a boil. Remove from the heat and sift in the flour, then stir to combine. Beat the mixture vigorously with a wooden spoon until it comes away from the sides of the saucepan, then allow to cool a little.

2 Add the eggs, a little at a time, until the mixture is soft and smooth and has a dropping consistency (you may not need to add all the egg).

3 Fit a size 8 plain round nozzle into a pastry bag and pipe small round mounds of the mixture onto a greased baking sheet. Bake in the preheated oven for 20–25 minutes. Remove and let cool.

4 Whisk the heavy cream with the confectioners' sugar until thick and fluffy. Cut a slit in the profiteroles and fill with the sweetened cream.

5 Melt the chocolate in a heatproof bowl set over a saucepan of simmering water, or in a microwave on full power for 1 minute. Stir in the butter, allow to melt, and combine to make a smooth mixture. Let cool slightly.

6 Spread a little of the chocolate mixture over the top of each profiterole with a narrow spatula. If desired, the profiteroles can be decorated to look like mice: add a pair of flaked almond ears, a chocolate chip nose, glacé cherry eyes, and a red licorice tail.

 Preparation/cooking
10 minutes/35 minutes plus decoration

 Oven temperature
400°F/200°C

 Makes 20 profiteroles

 Nutritional information
Rich source of vitamin A.

 Suitable for freezing
undecorated

—— TIP ——
The pastry will expand during cooking, so do not make the pastry for the profiterole mice longer than 1½ inches.

CHEWY APRICOT & CHOCOLATE CEREAL BARS

1¼ cups (150g) rolled oats

¼ cups (50g) puffed rice

½ cup (100g) dried apricots, chopped

½ cup (60g) pecans, chopped (optional)

7 tbsp (100g) unsalted butter

½ cup (125g) corn syrup

3oz (85g) white (or regular) chocolate

These are great for special treats and are popular with adults and children. They are fun for children to make themselves since they require no baking.

1 Combine the oats, puffed rice, chopped apricots, and nuts (if using) in a mixing bowl.

2 Put the butter and corn syrup in a small saucepan and heat gently. Add the chocolate and stir until melted. Stir the mixture into the dry ingredients until they are well coated.

3 Press the mixture firmly into a shallow 11 x 7in (28 x 18cm) lined pan using a potato masher to level the surface. Place in refrigerator to cool. Cut into bars and keep refrigerated.

 Preparation
15 minutes plus refrigeration time

 Makes 10 portions

 Nutritional information
Rich source of fiber, folic acid, iron, vitamin A, and vitamin B12.

MENUS: 4–6 months

START WITH ONE MEAL of solids a day, building up to three solid meals a day by week five or six, when a third solid meal should be introduced at dinnertime. It is a good idea to offer half the usual milk feeding before the solids, then finish the meal with milk (see page 24). Some babies may need an extra milk feeding or a little cooled boiled water during the day.

WEEKS 1&2	EARLY A.M.	BREAKFAST	LUNCH	MID P.M.	BEDTIME
DAY 1	MILK	MILK	MILK FIRST FRUIT PUREE (APPLE) *see page 29*	MILK	MILK
DAY 2	MILK	MILK	MILK FIRST VEG PUREE (CARROT) *see page 28*	MILK	MILK
DAY 3	MILK	MILK	MILK FRUITY INFANT RICE (PEAR) *see page 29*	MILK	MILK
DAY 4	MILK	MILK	MILK FIRST VEG PUREE (POTATO) *see page 28*	MILK	MILK
DAY 5	MILK	MILK	MILK FIRST FRUIT PUREE (APPLE) *see page 29*	MILK	MILK
DAY 6	MILK	MILK	MILK SWEET POTATO PUREE *see page 30*	MILK	MILK
DAY 7	MILK	MILK	MILK MASHED BANANA *see page 29*	MILK	MILK

WEEKS 3&4	EARLY A.M.	BREAKFAST	LUNCH	MID P.M.	BEDTIME
DAY 1	MILK	MILK FRUITY INFANT RICE (PEAR) *see page 29*	MILK FIRST VEG PUREE (CARROT) *see page 28*	MILK	MILK
DAY 2	MILK	MILK FIRST FRUIT PUREE (APPLE) *see page 29*	MILK FIRST VEG PUREE (POTATO) *see page 28*	MILK	MILK
DAY 3	MILK	MILK PEACH PUREE & INFANT RICE *see page 31*	MILK FIRST VEG PUREE (RUTABAGA) *see page 28*	MILK	MILK
DAY 4	MILK	MILK MASHED BANANA *see page 29*	MILK FIRST VEG PUREE (PARSNIP) *see page 28*	MILK	MILK
DAY 5	MILK	MILK FIRST FRUIT PUREE (PEAR) *see page 29*	MILK AVOCADO PUREE *see page 31*	MILK	MILK
DAY 6	MILK	MILK MASHED PAPAYA *see page 29*	MILK CREAMY VEG PUREE (CARROT) *see page 28*	MILK	MILK
DAY 7	MILK	MILK MASHED BANANA & PAPAYA *see page 29*	MILK FIRST VEG PUREE (POTATO) *see page 28*	MILK	MILK

MENUS: 6–9 months

YOU CAN NOW OFFER a wider variety of flavors and textures. Let your baby's appetite guide you as to how much milk you give with solid meals and whether you give one or two courses. I have made suggestions for simple desserts at lunchtime and you can include something similar at dinner if your baby still seems hungry after his main course.

	BREAKFAST	SNACK	LUNCH	SNACK	DINNER	BEDTIME
DAY 1	MILK CEREAL MASHED BANANA *see page 29*	MILK	POTATO, LEEK & PEA PUREE *see page 42* JUICE FIRST FRUIT PUREE (PEAR) *see page 29*	MILK	FISH WITH CARROTS & ORANGE *see page 46*	MILK
DAY 2	MILK DRIED APRICOTS WITH SEMOLINA *see page 42*	MILK	FIRST CHICKEN CASSEROLE *see page 47* JUICE FIRST FRUIT PUREE (APPLE) *see page 29*	MILK	TOMATO & CAULIFLOWER GRATIN WITH STEAMED CARROT STICKS *see page 44*	MILK
DAY 3	MILK CEREAL FIRST FRUIT PUREE (APPLE & PEAR) *see page 29*	MILK	BRAISED BEEF WITH CARROT, PARSNIP & POTATO *see page 47* FROMAGE FRAIS	MILK	PAPAYA & COTTAGE CHEESE *see page 40*	MILK
DAY 4	MILK WELL COOKED SCRAMBLED EGG WITH TOAST YOGURT	MILK	LENTIL & VEGETABLE PUREE *see page 43* PEACH PUREE WITH BABY RICE *see page 31*	MILK	TRIO OF ROOT VEGETABLES *see page 43*	MILK
DAY 5	MILK CEREAL	MILK	FLOUNDER FILLET WITH LEEK & CHEESE SAUCE *see page 45* PEACH, APPLE & STRAWBERRY PUREE *see page 41*	MILK	SWEET POTATO, CARROT & BROCCOLI *see page 44*	MILK
DAY 6	MILK APRICOT, PEAR, PEACH & APPLE COMPOTE *see page 41* FROMAGE FRAIS	MILK	PAPAYA & CHICKEN PUREE *see page 40* YOGURT	MILK	FILLET OF COD WITH A TRIO OF VEGETABLES *see page 45*	MILK
DAY 7	MILK CEREAL WITH MILK MASHED PAPAYA OR BANANA *see page 29*	MILK	CAULIFLOWER GRATIN (VARIATION) *see page 44* CHUNKS OF SOFT, RIPE FRUIT E.G., PEAR OR PEACH	MILK	SPINACH, POTATO, PARSNIP & LEEK *see page 44*	MILK

MENUS: 9–12 months

MOST OF THESE RECIPES are found in the 9–12 month section, but dishes from previous chapters are also suitable. You can substitute a selection of finger foods, such as strips of roast chicken, cheese, fruit, and rice cakes, for cooked meals. Serve the snacks with a drink of milk between main meals, perhaps mid-morning and mid-afternoon.

	BREAKFAST	LUNCH	DINNER	SNACKS
DAY 1	FRUITY BABY MUESLI *see page 57* YOGURT	QUICK CHICKEN COUSCOUS *see page 60* FRUIT	CHEESY PASTA STARS *see page 58* EXOTIC FRUIT SALAD *see page 57*	MILK SANDWICHES *see page 89* DRIED FRUIT
DAY 2	SCRAMBLED EGG WITH TOAST FIRST FRUIT PUREE (APPLE) *see page 29*	FILLET OF FISH MORNAY WITH VEGETABLES *see page 59* FRUIT	PASTA WITH TOMATO & MASCARPONE SAUCE *see page 58* FRUIT	MILK VEGETABLE FINGERS AND TOAST STRIPS WITH DIPS YOGURT
DAY 3	CEREAL FRUIT FROMAGE FRAIS	BABY'S BOLOGNESE *see page 61* FRUIT	EASY MASHED VEGETABLE DUO *see page 56* BANANA	MILK SANDWICHES *see page 89* GRATED APPLE
DAY 4	TOAST WITH A SAVORY SPREAD OR JAM FRUIT	FLAKED COD WITH TOMATOES & ZUCCHINI *see page 60* YOGURT	CREAMY CHICKEN & BROCCOLI *see page 61* FRUIT	MILK VEGETABLE FINGERS AND CHEESE STICKS DRIED FRUIT
DAY 5	APPLE & DATE OATMEAL *see page 57* FRUIT	FRUITY CHICKEN WITH CARROTS *see page 61* FROMAGE FRAIS	CHEESY PASTA STARS *see page 58* APPLE PUREE *see page 29*	MILK SANDWICHES *see page 89* FRUIT
DAY 6	RAISIN TOAST FINGERS APPLE & PEAR PUREE *see page 29*	BRAISED BEEF WITH CARROT, PARSNIP & POTATO *see page 47* YOGURT	STEAMED VEGETABLE FINGERS AND CHEESE STICKS FRUIT	MILK CHEESE ON TOAST FRUIT
DAY 7	CEREAL JUICY PEAR & PRUNE PUREE *see page 41*	CALIFORNIA CHICKEN *see page 60* FRUIT	CAULIFLOWER GRATIN (VARIATION) *see page 44* FRUIT	MILK SANDWICHES *see page 89* YOGURT

MENUS: 12–18 months

YOUR CHILD is now able to join in family meals and many of these recipes are suitable for the whole family. Choose your preferred accompaniments to main courses, perhaps pasta, potatoes, bread, or rice, and a selection of vegetables. Your child should also drink at least ⅔ pint (400ml) of milk daily, which can be given with his snacks.

	BREAKFAST	LUNCH	DINNER	SNACKS
DAY 1	TOAST WITH SAVORY SPREAD OR JAM YOGURT FRUIT	TURKEY BALLS & PEPPER SAUCE see page 76 FRUIT	ORZO WITH COLORFUL DICED VEGETABLES see page 73 APRICOT & PEAR PUREE see page 31	MILK SANDWICHES see page 89 YOGURT
DAY 2	CEREAL FROMAGE FRAIS FRUIT	SHEPHERD'S PIE see page 77 RASPBERRY FROZEN YOGURT see page 78	ZUCCHINI & TOMATO FRITTATA see page 70 FRUIT	MILK TOASTED HAM AND CHEESE SANDWICH DRIED FRUIT
DAY 3	SCRAMBLED EGG WITH TOAST FRUIT	CHICKEN SAUSAGE SNAIL see page 75 YOGURT	PASTA CARTWHEELS (VARIATION) see page 71 BANANA	MILK CREAMY AVOCADO DIP & VEGETABLE FINGERS see page 56 FRUIT
DAY 4	APRICOT & BLUEBERRY OATMEAL see page 70 YOGURT	MINI PIZZA see page 91 FRUIT SALAD	TUNA & ZUCCHINI LASAGNA see page 72 FRUIT	MILK BAKED BEANS WITH TOAST FROMAGE FRAIS AND FRUIT
DAY 5	BOILED EGG WITH FINGERS OF TOAST FROMAGE FRAIS FRUIT	FINGER PICKING CHICKEN & POTATO BALLS see page 77 BANANA	PASTA WITH TOMATO & MASCARPONE SAUCE see page 58	MILK VEGETABLE FINGERS AND OTHER FINGER FOODS ICE CREAM
DAY 6	CEREAL YOGURT AND FRUIT	BOW-TIE PASTA WITH HAM & PEAS see page 73 FRUIT	FRITTATA see page 70 FRUIT	MILK BAKED BEANS WITH TOAST BANANA
DAY 7	YOGURT PANCAKES WITH MAPLE SYRUP see page 78 FRUIT	PASTA CARTWHEELS WITH CHEESE & BROCCOLI see page 71 ICE CREAM	JOY'S FISH PIE see page 74 FRUIT	MILK BREAD STICKS WITH CHUNKY TOMATO & CREAM CHEESE DIP see page 88 DRIED FRUIT

MENUS: 18 months–2 years

SHARED FAMILY MEALS are not always possible, so
I have included recipes that can be prepared in
advance or frozen so that your toddler can eat
the same food as you but at an earlier time. At this age,
most children tend not to eat much at one sitting, so
between-meal snacks with milk are especially important.

	BREAKFAST	LUNCH	DINNER	SNACKS
DAY 1	CEREAL CHEESE FRUIT	ANNABEL'S VEGETABLE CROQUETTES *see page 94* HOMEMADE ICE POP *see page 99*	CHICKEN BOLOGNESE *see page 97* FRUIT	MILK SANDWICHES *see page 89* YOGURT
DAY 2	SCRAMBLED EGG WITH CHEESE & TOMATO *see page 88* FIRST FRUIT PUREE (APPLE) *see page 29*	BOW-TIE PASTA WITH SPRING VEGETABLES *see page 90* FRUIT	SHEPHERD'S PIE *see page 77* FRUIT	MILK BAKED BEANS WITH TOAST FROMAGE FRAIS
DAY 3	APRICOT & BLUEBERRY OATMEAL *see page 70* YOGURT	ALPHABET PASTA MINESTRONE *see page 90* FRUIT	SALMON STARFISH *see page 95* FRUIT	MILK CHEESE ON TOAST DRIED FRUIT AND RICE CAKES
DAY 4	CEREAL STRAWBERRY & BANANA SMOOTHIE *see page 98*	LAMB MEATBALLS WITH A SWEET & SOUR SAUCE *see page 97* RASPBERRY FROZEN YOGURT *see page 78*	MULTICOLORED RICE WITH KIDNEY BEANS *see page 92* FRUIT	MILK RAISIN & OATMEAL COOKIES *see page 98* FRUIT
DAY 5	APPLE, MANGO & APRICOT MUESLI *see page 88* YOGURT	MINI PIZZAS *see page 91* JELL-O AND ICE CREAM	CHICKEN KABOBS WITH HONEY & CITRUS MARINADE *see page 96* FRUIT	MILK RAW VEGETABLES AND OTHER FINGER FOODS BANANA MUFFIN *see page 98*
DAY 6	BANANA MUFFIN *see page 98* FROMAGE FRAIS FRUIT	CHICKEN SAUSAGE SNAIL *see page 75* FRUIT	ZUCCHINI & TOMATO FRITTATA *see page 70* MOCK FRIED EGG MADE WITH VANILLA YOGURT AND APRICOT *see page 103*	MILK SANDWICHES *see page 89* FRUIT
DAY 7	TOAST WITH SAVORY SPREAD OR JAM FRUIT YOGURT AND HONEY	CORN, CHERRY TOMATO & TOFU KABOB *see page 92* FRUIT	ONE-POT RICE WITH CHICKEN *see page 96* FRUIT	MILK SARDINES ON TOAST STRAWBERRY & BANANA SMOOTHIE *see page 98*

MENUS: 2–3 years

THIS MENU PLAN shows a progressively wider choice of recipes that will accustom your child to new tastes. As with the other menu charts, you can substitute a few healthy convenience foods, such as pizzas, cooked chicken pieces, or fish fingers, and vary or omit desserts, but try to keep snacks nutritious and provide milk, fruit juice, or water.

	BREAKFAST	LUNCH	DINNER	SNACKS
DAY 1	APPLE, MANGO & APRICOT MUESLI *see page 88* YOGURT AND HONEY	PASTA WITH ZUCCHINI, PEPPERS & SAUSAGES *see page 109* FRUIT AND ICE CREAM	TERIYAKI CHICKEN STIR-FRY *see page 111* FROMAGE FRAIS	MILK SANDWICHES *see page 89* FRUIT
DAY 2	BOILED EGG WITH FINGERS OF TOAST FRUIT FROMAGE FRAIS	TOMATO SOUP *see page 106* FRUIT	ANNABEL'S TASTY MEATBALLS *see page 112* ICE CREAM	MILK BANANA MUFFIN *see page 98* PLAIN YOGURT AND HONEY
DAY 3	CEREAL CHEESE FRUIT	BOW-TIE PASTA WITH HAM & PEAS *see page 73* SALAD JELL-O AND ICE CREAM	VEGETABLE LASAGNA *see page 109* FRUIT	MILK BAKED BEANS WITH TOAST FRUIT
DAY 4	OATMEAL RAISIN TOAST FRUIT	ANNABEL'S VEGETABLE CROQUETTES *see page 94* STICKY TOFFEE PUDDING *see page 113*	GOLDEN TURKEY FINGERS *see page 110* YOGURT	MILK CHEESE AND VEGETABLE STICKS FRUIT
DAY 5	TOAST WITH SAVORY SPREAD OR JAM YOGURT FRUIT	HEART-SHAPED CHICKEN NUGGETS *see page 110* FRUIT	ANNABEL'S PASTA SALAD *see page 108* RAW VEGETABLES & DIP ICE CREAM	MILK RAISIN & OATMEAL COOKIE *see page 98* CHOCOLATE SMOOTHIE *see page 98*
DAY 6	CEREAL YOGURT FRUIT	GOLDEN TURKEY FINGERS *see page 110* RAISIN & OATMEAL COOKIES *see page 98*	HUNGARIAN GOULASH *see page 112* FRUIT	MILK CHEESE ON TOAST DRIED FRUIT
DAY 7	SCRAMBLED EGG WITH TOAST FRUIT	CARAMELIZED CHICKEN BREAST *see page 110* FRUIT	MINI BAKED POTATO *see page 107* SALAD FRUIT	MILK SANDWICHES *see page 89* HOMEMADE ICE POP *see page 99*

MENUS: 3–5 years

AT THIS AGE, children love to help prepare their meals
and there are many simple things they can do, like
cut sandwich shapes. Although I have suggested fruit
after most meals, it is fine to offer occasional treats like cake
or cookies. If your child eats lunch at nursery or preschool,
just balance her evening meal at home accordingly.

	BREAKFAST	LUNCH	DINNER	SNACKS
DAY 1	POACHED OR FRIED EGG WITH FINGERS OF TOAST CEREAL FRUIT	SPAGHETTI WITH SPECIAL TOMATO SAUCE *see page 122* SALAD FRUIT	PAELLA *see page 126* FRUIT	MILK VEGETABLE STICKS WITH HUMMUS BANANA MUFFIN *see page 98*
DAY 2	APPLE, MANGO & APRICOT MUESLI *see page 88* YOGURT FRUIT	BEEF TERIYAKI SKEWERS *see page 129* SALAD FRUIT	ITALIAN RISOTTO WITH MUSHROOMS & PEAS *see page 123* ICE CREAM FRUIT	MILK CHEESE ON TOAST CHEWY APRICOT & CEREAL BAR *see page 131*
DAY 3	OATMEAL WITH HONEY OR JAM THINLY SLICED CHEESE OR MINIATURE CHEESES FRUIT	STICKY BAR-B-Q DRUMSTICKS *see page 126* RASPBERRY FROZEN YOGURT *see page 78*	SINGAPORE NOODLES *see page 128* EXOTIC FRUIT SALAD *see page 57*	MILK BAKED BEANS WITH TOAST CHOCOLATE CHIP & ORANGE CUT-OUT COOKIES *see page 130*
DAY 4	SCRAMBLED EGG WITH CHEESE & TOMATO *see page 88* TOAST FRUIT	CHICKEN SATAY *see page 127* FRUIT	FISH & OVEN-BAKED FRIES *see page 125* JELL-O AND ICE CREAM	MILK SANDWICHES *see page 89* FRUIT
DAY 5	YOGURT PANCAKES WITH MAPLE SYRUP *see page 78* FROMAGE FRAIS FRUIT	MINI BAKED POTATOES *see page 107* FRUIT	BEEF STIR-FRY WITH OYSTER SAUCE *see page 128* STICKY TOFFEE PUDDING *see page 113*	MILK VEGETABLE AND CHEESE STICKS RAISIN & OATMEAL COOKIES *see page 98*
DAY 6	CEREAL CHEESE FRUIT	MINI BEAN & VEGGIE ENCHILADAS *see page 125* FRUIT	CHICKEN BOLOGNESE *see page 97* JELL-O & ICE CREAM	MILK SANDWICHES *see page 89* DRIED FRUIT FROMAGE FRAIS
DAY 7	WAFFLE & MAPLE SYRUP FRUIT YOGURT	EGG-FRIED RICE WITH CHICKEN & SHRIMP *see page 127*	MILDLY SPICED VEGETABLE SAMOSAS *see page 124* FRUIT	MILK COUNTRY APPLE CAKE *see page 130* FRUIT

Snacks & Party Food

SNACKS ARE AN IMPORTANT part of young children's diets. Encourage them to eat well now and you will have the basis for a lifetime of healthy eating. For special meals, such as a birthday, you could make up an individual picnic box for each child.

HEALTHY SNACKS

RECIPES FOR SNACKS

STRAWBERRY & BANANA SMOOTHIE
see page 98

CHUNKY TOMATO
& CREAM CHEESE DIP/CREAMY AVOCADO
DIP & VEGETABLE FINGERS
see pages 88 and 56

MOCK FRIED EGG
(VANILLA YOGURT & CANNED PEACH HALF)
see page 103

RAISIN & OATMEAL COOKIES
see page 98

BANANA MUFFINS
see page 98

HOMEMADE ICE POPS
see page 99

RASPBERRY FROZEN YOGURT
see page 78

ROOT VEGETABLE CHIPS
see page 70

SANDWICHES
see page 89

SCRAMBLED EGGS WITH CHEESE & TOMATO
see page 88

MIXED SALAD WITH DRESSING FROM
ANNABEL'S PASTA SALAD
see page 108

OTHER IDEAS

BOILED EGG WITH FINGERS OF TOAST; FRENCH BREAD;
CHEESE ON TOAST; TOASTED RAISIN BREAD
FINGERS WITH CREAM CHEESE; TOASTED SANDWICHES
(E.G., HAM & CHEESE); MINIATURE CHEESES & CHEESE SLICES;
DRIED FRUIT; FRESH FRUIT & FRUIT SALAD;
WHOLE GRAIN BREAKFAST CEREAL WITH MILK; BAKED
BEANS ON TOAST; GLASS OF MILK OR FRESH ORANGE JUICE;
POPCORN; YOGURT; RICE CAKES; CRISPBREADS;
BREAD STICKS; VEGETABLES (E.G., CARROTS, CUCUMBER,
CHERRY TOMATOES, CELERY, ON THEIR OWN OR WITH A DIP)

PARTY PLANNER

PREPARE IN ADVANCE

PACKAGE BIRTHDAY CAKE
see page 115

HEART-SHAPED CHICKEN NUGGETS
see page 110

CHUNKY TOMATO & CREAM CHEESE DIP
(CUT CRUDITÉS THE DAY BEFORE THE PARTY)
see page 88

CHARACTER CAKES
(DECORATE THE DAY BEFORE THE PARTY)
see page 114

CHOCOLATE PUFF PASTRY MICE
(DECORATE THE DAY BEFORE THE PARTY)
see page 131

CHEWY APRICOT & CEREAL BARS
see page 131

JELL-O BOATS
(CUT IN HALF AND DECORATE ON THE DAY)
see page 79

SHORTBREAD COOKIES
see page 115

MAKE ON THE DAY

SANDWICH SELECTION
see page 89

ANNABEL'S PASTA SALAD
see page 108

CHICKEN KABOBS
WITH HONEY & CITRUS MARINADE
see page 96

CHICKEN SATAY
see page 127

PASTA WITH
ZUCCHINI, PEPPERS & SAUSAGES
see page 109

GOLDEN TURKEY FINGERS
see page 110

MINI PIZZAS
see page 91

FRESH FRUIT PLATTER
WITH CHOCOLATE-DIPPED FRUIT

Index

Acknowledgments

Author's Acknowledgments

I am indebted to the following people for their help and advice during the writing of this book: Dr. Margaret Lawson, Senior Lecturer in Pediatric Nutrition, Institute of Child Health; Dr. Stephen Herman FRCP, Consultant Pediatrician, Central Middlesex Hospital; Dr. Barry Lewis FRCP, FRCPH Consultant Pediatrician; Luci Daniels, State Registered Dietitian; Simon Karmel; David Karmel; Evelyn Etkind; Jane Hamilton; Marian Magpoc; Letty Catada; Jo Pratt; Joy Skipper; Jacqui Morley; Lara Tankel. I would especially like to thank Nicholas, Lara, and Scarlett Karmel, and all the other discerning young tasters who have eaten their way through the recipes in this book. Thanks also to photographer Ian O'Leary, and the members of the DK team who have worked on this project.

Dorling Kindersley would like to thank: Dr. Margaret Lawson for advice on nutrition; Jasmine Challis for the nutritional analyses; Dave King for additional photography; Emma Brogi for photographic assistance; Sue Henderson for food styling on pages 86–7; Lorraine Turner and Alrica Green for editorial work; Hilary Bird for the index.

Many thanks to all our models:

Connor Bailey, Sam Bower, Nicoletta Comand and Melisande Croft, Laurie Claxton, Sophie Crook, Liam and Katie Dalmon, Page Fairclough (Bubblegum Agency), Abigail and Matthew Freathy, Harriet Hayles (Bubblegum Agency), Rosie Johnson, Scarlett Karmel, Alexander and Charlotte Kay, Peter Kelleher, Iris Mathieson, Georgina and Jack McCooke, Max Moore, Eleni Neophitou, Elicia Oliver-Knox, Elise Palmer, Kyle Perry, Joshua Richardson, Holly and Claire Robinson, Ellie-Louise Thomson.

Photography credits

Recipe photography by Ian O'Leary, except pp. 86-7 by Dave King. Other food photography by Ian O'Leary, Andy Crawford, Clive Streeter, and Dave King.
Model photography by Andy Crawford, except pp.9–11 by Steve Gorton; p.15, tl, p.67 and p.82, tr, Dave King; p.15, tr, Steve Shott; page 22, bl, Jenny Matthews; p.24, br, Susanna Price; p. 32 and p.33, tr, Julie Fisher; p.34, tr, p.52, bl, p.64, tl, and p.33, tl, Jo Foord.

Useful Addresses

National Health Information Center
PO Box 1133,
Washington, DC 20013.
Tel: (800) 336-4797

La Leche League International
1400 N. Meacham Rd.,
Schaumburg, IL 60173–4048.
Tel: (847) 519–7730

American Academy of Pediatrics
141 Northwest Point Blvd.,
Elk Grove Village, IL 60007.
Tel: (800) 433-9016

Healthy Mothers, Healthy Babies Coalition
Tel: (800) 673-8444

American Dietetic Association
216 W. Jackson Blvd.,
Chicago, IL 60606–6995.
Tel: (312) 899–0040/
    (800) 877–1600
Fax: (312) 899–1979

American Academy of Pediatric Dentistry
211 E. Chicago Avenue,
Suite 700,
Chicago, IL 60611–2616.
Tel: (312) 337–2169

Food and Drug Administration
Office of Consumer Affairs,
5600 Fishers Lane,
Rockville, MD 20857.
Tel: (301) 443–1544

HELPFUL WEBSITES
Parents Place
www.parentsplace.com

Food Allergy Network
www.foodallergy.com

Parents of Allergic Children
drone.simplenet.com/pac

Alternative Health
www.healthychild.com

American School Food Service (ASFSA)
www.asfsa.org

National Health Information Center
www.nhic-nt.health.org

American Academy of Pediatrics
www.aap.org

American Dietetic Association
www.eatright.org

La Leche League International
www.lalecheleague.org